Inside Advice On
MARKETING SENIOR HOUSING

Reviews

Inside Advice On
MARKETING SENIOR HOUSING
The 15 Critical Components of
SUCCESS

Phyllis Thornton and Christine Wirthwein have published the first "how-to" senior housing marketing compendium, based on their collective history of success, that is intelligent, forthright, and street savvy. From the very first chapter, *Inside Advice on Marketing Senior Housing* offers endless pearls and straight-line formulas for those who are beginning and inside advice for the especially experienced professional. There's even a *Marketing Plan Template* on CD.

Don't be fooled by the title into thinking this is a book only for the marketing professional. *Inside Advice on Marketing Senior Housing* is a smart purchase for anyone who manages senior housing communities. Too often, the executive director or chief executive officer isn't knowledgeable about the very foundation of the organization's revenue stream. This leader often lacks assessment skills—or even the basic language of marketing. Leadership also tends to shy away from the tension between the marketing office and other operating departments. Trouble brews from a lack of understanding of, and an appreciation for, how interdependent operations and marketing are. Ensuring that each department head gains access to *Inside Advice on Marketing Senior Housing* can go a long way to resolving these tensions. It offers an avenue of knowledge that leads to more effective teamwork.

The confidence expressed in this straightforward read is both reassuring and inspiring in a competitive marketplace where future success is in the balance and where precious dollars are set aside from tight operations budgets. Hopefully, every senior housing community will have one or more copies of *Inside Advice on Marketing Senior Housing* eventually frayed at the corners and sagging from use. Those organizations who understand there truly is no maintaining any longer, only growth, whether at a single site or within a system, will seize this opportunity to learn from the wealth of experience Phyllis and Christine bring to such a critical topic. This book is long overdue.

Robert M. Alston
President & Chief Executive Officer
Friendship Senior Options, Inc.
Friendship Village of Schaumburg Parent Company

For senior housing providers to be successful year in and year out, they must have a marketing plan and program that every employee, not just the marketing staff, takes on as his or her own. Such a program becomes a way of life for staff in meeting the ever-increasing challenges of maintaining a competitive edge in the marketplace. If you really want to learn how to turn your community into a powerhouse, where every staff member understands the power of his or her daily "marketing" presence within the community, I highly recommend this publication to you.

Inside Advice on Marketing Senior Housing—The 15 Critical Components of Success has been developed by two of the most respected and successful innovators in marketing senior housing communities. They have combined their talents and energies to give us the gift of their vast experience in an easy-to-apply strategy for marketing success.

JOSEPH L. BENSON, RHPF
President
Wyndemere Senior Living Campus

I started out in the industry 14 years ago as that inexperienced young kid with a marketing degree who is described in Chapter Four of *Inside Advice on Marketing Senior Housing*. I found myself in a job with no manual, no textbook, and no idea of how to market a retirement community. I struggled for a couple of years, running the same old ad in the local newspaper and having those "cheerful open houses."

As I continued to see occupancy rates drop, a card came in the mail advertising a marketing seminar and Phyllis Thornton was the featured speaker. It was one of those days that you say to yourself, "I need to attend, but who has time? I'm too busy trying to fill these apartments!" When the card reappeared, I decided to attend, and discovered all the things I was doing wrong, and then learned what to do right. I later worked with Phyllis to develop a marketing plan that I use to this day. I refer to it as my "marketing bible." Today, Park Central maintains 98% occupancy in the midst of a competitive marketplace.

The information presented in *Inside Advice on Marketing Senior Housing* now makes it possible for other retirement communities to enjoy the same success. It lays out a step-by-step program to reach and maintain your occupancy goals. No retirement community should go into a master planning process without first having these proven strategies in place.

Inside Advice on Marketing Senior Housing is the best investment you will ever make to ensure the success of your community and your profession.

PAULA BLISS
Assistant Vice President Marketing
Park Central Retirement Community

Inside Advice on Marketing Senior Housing—The 15 Critical Components of Success is the best resource for senior living marketing I have ever read! It's a must for success-oriented people and communities.

DENNIS BOZZI
President
Life Services Network

At last, there is a comprehensive, easy-to-follow book about how to market senior housing the right way. I plan to furnish copies of *Inside Advice on Marketing Senior Housing* to all our leadership staff and I recommend other boards do the same. Phyllis Thornton and Christine Wirthwein have given their readers all of the necessary knowledge, tools, and motivation to successfully market with ease, skill, and confidence.

SUSIE BUSS
Board Member
Hamilton Communities

As the senior housing industry becomes more competitive and new players enter the market, it is essential for marketing directors and sales staff to become more educated and adept. However, until now, there was no one source from which to obtain all the information needed. Most marketing directors rely on seminars or conferences that may or may not provide adequate information. Some organizations engage consultants to provide training for their marketing staff. Networking and information sharing is another common way of learning. The Life Services Network Marketing Professional Certification Program (MPCP), which I attended in 1998, is perhaps the only option that provides the essentials of marketing senior housing. Now *Inside Advice on Marketing Senior Housing* brings all the information and expertise of the MPCP to a broader audience.

As an 11-year veteran of the marketing profession, I've had the opportunity to work with both Phyllis Thornton and Christine Wirthwein. I know first hand that the proven methods presented by these two seasoned professionals are based on their many years of development and implementation experience in a variety of communities. Their combined knowledge has come together in this comprehensive, yet easy-to-read book.

Finally, we have a complete guide and a step-by-step process for achieving marketing success in senior housing!

ROSEMARY CICAK, MGS, CMP
Vice President of Marketing & Public Relations
Otterbein Homes, Inc.

So often we hire marketing personnel and wonder, "How do I build their expertise, knowledge, and effectiveness within the organization?" Some of our choices are to allow staff to learn on their own initiative, to flounder as they learn slowly from experience, to send them to a fast-paced marketing seminar, or to hire an expensive industry marketing consultant to provide staff support.

Inside Advice on Marketing Senior Housing—The 15 Critical Components of Success is the answer to this dilemma. Created by two of the most accomplished marketing leaders in our industry, it's a highly valuable resource for the novice or experienced marketer and provides clear-cut advice that can easily be put into practice in any organization. What a refreshing alternative to the other fruitless training and education choices!

H. DAVID CLAUS
President & Chief Executive Officer
Holland Home

Marketing has become one of the most enigmatic aspects of developing and managing senior adult facilities and programs. The confusion is compounded by the many individuals who are attracted to the opportunities in a rapidly growing seniors' market, and who attempt to retrofit their marketing skills from other careers. The welcomed, but somewhat opportunistic newcomers "cut and paste" their general experiences into the field of aging, whether they fit or not. This approach is akin to that old saying: "The trouble with being a hammer is that everything you see looks like a nail."

Phyllis Thornton and Christine Wirthwein are a breath of fresh air in the frenzy. They teach and coach an approach that keeps marketing tasks simple, functional, and understandable for practitioners both seasoned and new. *Inside Advice on Marketing Senior Housing* is a must read!

KENNETH T. DURAND
President & Chief Executive Officer
C.C. Young

How to spend money on marketing is a subject often misunderstood. It's an investment, not an expense, and a systematic funding approach that pays dividends in the form of high occupancy and protection of the organization's financial stability. *Inside Advice on Marketing Senior Housing—The 15 Critical Components of Success* is a must read for board and staff. It provides comprehensive and definitive direction on how to establish a marketing program that uses all the right resources and ensures the highest return.

MICHAEL A. FLYNN
Chief Executive Officer
Smith Senior Living

Phyllis and Christine have come down from the mountaintop with tablets containing 15 marketing commandments. They have produced an invigorating book, chock-full of material based on years of experience garnered in the "tactical trenches" of marketing, not taught in the classroom. The *Template* contained on the accompanying CD is a virtual "how-to" on developing a marketing plan. They correctly see the essence of marketing as the "quality of the product" and customer service as "how you communicate that quality." This is their mantra.

Inside Advice on Marketing Senior Housing—The 15 Critical Components of Success should be required reading not only for marketing professionals, but also for anyone who manages or operates a senior living community.

BRIAN E. FORSCHNER, PH.D.
President
Senior Health & Housing Services
Mercy Health Partners

Many individuals in our profession don't have formal training in marketing senior housing. They have the heart, but not the know-how. When I assumed my present position, I bought at least a dozen books in search of how to do my job. Each book had some information that helped, but *Inside Advice on Marketing Senior Housing* is exactly what I needed. Its easy, no-nonsense style, along with step-by-step instruction, is excellent.

It is obvious that Phyllis Thornton and Christine Wirthwein have experience in what they are talking about.

CONNIE GARBER
Vice President
Community-Based Services
Greencroft Retirement Communities

Inside Advice on Marketing Senior Housing—The 15 Critical Components of Success is a very practical guide to developing a successful marketing program. I have experienced the results first hand! These components, when implemented effectively, result in an inspired team that is able to capture today's senior housing opportunities.

BOB HAUSMANN
Partner
Director of Active Adult/Senior Housing
Miller Valentine Group

Finding resources that are both affordable and appropriate for the marketing staff at our nine communities has been a challenge. The information and direction provided in *Inside Advice on Marketing Senior Housing* is clear, concise, and adaptable to each community and its unique situation. The materials are comprehensive and outline a tool for evaluating the marketing program for any community. When I began marketing senior living communities more than 13 years ago, this book would have been extremely helpful in giving a more successful focus to our early years. Thanks to Phyllis and Christine for putting together their wealth of knowledge.

MARCIA S. HEMPEL
Administrator of Marketing
Lutheran Senior Services

Inside Advice on Marketing Senior Housing is an excellent compilation of the nuts and bolts of marketing senior living and provides helpful insights for marketing professionals as well as other key administrative staff. It challenges traditional thinking in a number of areas, with the clear goal of raising the bar for all senior living providers. Whether you're self-managing your marketing services or you've hired marketing experts to assist, this book provides wisdom and objective measures for bringing your organization to a stronger market, and ultimately, a stronger financial position.

DANIEL J. HERMANN
Managing Director & Group Head
Ziegler Capital Markets Group

Inside Advice on Marketing Senior Housing reads as if it were written for the marketing director, because this position leads and directs the bulk of the efforts the book details. However, *Inside Advice on Marketing Senior Housing* is not just for marketing staff. It is also written for the chief executive officer, chief operating officer, executive director, or administrator who has been in this field long enough to know how critical a good marketing effort is to the success of their senior housing communities.

The content makes it clear that no organization can succeed in marketing without involving the staff of every department. These staff make the marketing message real by practicing good customer service every time they interact with the public. The staff that clean apartments, maintain the grounds, answer phones, or provide food service do more in one day to affect the marketability of a facility than the marketing staff can collectively do in a month. The marketing department's best efforts can be made worthless by lack of support for its efforts or lack of customer service oriented behavior by other departments.

In fishing parlance, although it is the marketing staff that brings the prospective resident to the boat, it is the efforts of the rest of the organization's departments that make it possible to get the prospective resident into the boat.

Inside Advice On Marketing Senior Housing is one of the most detailed works I have ever read on this subject. It provides a comprehensive blueprint of the work in the trenches and the heavy lifting necessary to get the job done. If your staff are committed to the superior customer service described in this book, and your marketing staff use its techniques, you will reap the success your senior housing community deserves.

GREG HOLM
Chief Operating Officer & Executive Vice President
Ohio Masonic Home

Reading *Inside Advice on Marketing Senior Housing* made me feel like Popeye after he's guzzled down his can of spinach . . . charged with the strength and ability to make things happen and succeed! It's like having a personal coach or mentor sitting across the table guiding you each step of the way. Direct, succinct—even the tough concepts are easy to grasp and implement.

Finally, a bible for our industry! A must have and must read for anyone in marketing, sales, or administration.

RANDALYNN KAYE, CMP
Director of Marketing & Sales
Wyndemere Senior Living Campus

Inside Advice on Marketing Senior Housing—The 15 Critical Components of Success is the best and most comprehensive tool on "how-to-market" to the mature market that I have encountered in my 30-plus years in the profession.

What sets this book apart is that the material is organized in an easy-to-read manner and flows from topic to topic smoothly. The information is not pie-in-the-sky, but the real nuts and bolts of how to be successful in marketing to seniors. Thornton and Wirthwein don't shy away from dealing with issues that others gloss over or ignore, specifically as it pertains to helping all staff understand that they are an integral part of the marketing team and that customer service of the highest magnitude must be the norm.

The action steps and worksheets in the *Marketing Plan Template* are easy to follow and designed to be useful for the start-up project as well as the mature property trying to maintain market share.

THOMAS L. KELLY
Chief Executive Officer
Village On The Isle

Inside Advice on Marketing Senior Housing has more than captured the essence of marketing—it's the roadmap for newcomers to the field, and it serves as a resource for seasoned professionals to revisit some of the real issues that challenge us in this highly competitive, yet rewarding industry. The presentation of the information is well organized, practical, even fun—making it an easy read. I would highly recommend it for the CEO, COO, and CFO as well. *Inside Advice on Marketing Senior Housing* is a book that will hold a high place of prominence and honor in my professional library.

JUDITH K. LEWIS, RHP, CMP
Vice President of Marketing
Fairview Ministries, Inc.

An excellent, educational, and common sense approach to marketing! *Inside Advice on Marketing Senior Housing* not only reinforces the importance of a scientific approach to in-depth analysis and strategic planning, but also addresses the art of customer satisfaction as it relates to the frontline staff. It presents the comprehensive skills and concepts mandatory for the entire spectrum of senior housing. This book should be required reading for any manager who works with senior adults.

PEARL MERRITT, ED.D., MS, MSN, RN
Vice President
Buckner Retirement Services, Inc.

As a former marketing professional, it was no surprise to me as a CCRC board member to experience marketing as the driving force of our organization. It was a surprise, however, to realize there was no definitive marketing "textbook" to use as our guide and compass. Until now!

Inside Advice on Marketing Senior Housing is written with confidence—no timidity here. It brings the perspective of experience, not theory, and it's written in language the experienced marketer, as well as the average board member, can understand and use. Although our marketing team is one of the best in the business, I'll highly recommend this comprehensive resource to staff and board members alike. Thanks Phyllis and Christine—you've given the industry a great gift.

MERSHON NIESNER
Chair, Board of Directors
Friendship Senior Options, Inc.
Friendship Village of Schaumburg Parent Company

Instead of fancy approaches or high level strategies that may or may not connect with the real world, *Inside Advice on Marketing Senior Housing* puts the "cookies on the lower shelf" and within reach of those seeking marketing guidance pertaining to our industry. The down-home, fireside-chat approach is both refreshing and focused. The work is to be applauded for its heartfelt passion and concern for practical strategies and applications.

RICHARD W. OLSON
President & Chief Executive Officer
Fairview Ministries, Inc.

I absolutely appreciate this marketing resource more than the writers will ever know. Most marketing directors and counselors step into their roles coming from other disciplines, learning as they go. I wish I'd had this book when I assumed the role of director of marketing 10 years ago. *Inside Advice on Marketing Senior Housing* would have also supported what I learned in the Retirement Housing Professionals (RHP) program and the Marketing Professional Certification Program (MPCP). Christine and Phyllis have done a superb job of putting together must-know information for those who market retirement communities. Thank you!

SANDRA H. SMITH, RHP, CMP
Director of Marketing
Appalachian Christian Village, Inc.

In a profession where marketing becomes more and more complex and confusing each day, this book serves as an excellent guide for developing an effective, common sense approach to marketing senior housing. Its authors' many years of experience and expertise are presented in a down-to-earth approach that balances facts with practicality. It is well organized and a quick and easy read, providing enough detail without volumes of information that become unmanageable.

Inside Advice on Marketing Senior Housing—The 15 Critical Components of Success is a great resource for senior housing veterans and novices alike. In fact, I'm prepared to order several copies right now for my marketing team!

DUSTIN SCHOLZ
Director for Housing & Marketing
The Evangelical Lutheran Good Samaritan Society

There are many good managers and directors in the senior housing industry, however, there are very few marketing masters. Not because these individuals do not possess talent, but because they have never been taught how to master the art and science of marketing. Phyllis Thornton and Christine Wirthwein, the industry's foremost marketing masterminds, have changed that. With *Inside Advice on Marketing Senior Housing*, both new and experienced industry professionals now have the opportunity to become strategic-thinking experts.

Inside Advice on Marketing Senior Housing is not just a reference guide; the 15 critical components discussed in the book collectively form the building blocks of a solid and strategic campaign. The components are explained in an easy-to-read and interesting format, and the *Marketing Plan Template* is an exceptional tool that can be adapted by all marketing professionals to assist with their annual planning.

I've been extremely fortunate to have learned from and worked with both Phyllis and Christine. Their years of experience and deep knowledge of the industry have provided them with dynamic marketing methods that are successful time and time again. Don't set this book on your desk and refer to it periodically—read it, learn the concepts, and apply them to your marketing efforts. You will not be sorry.

MARK A. ZULLO, RHP, CMP
Director of Marketing & Sales
Life Care Retirement Communities, Inc.

Inside Advice On
MARKETING SENIOR HOUSING
The 15 Critical Components of
SUCCESS

Phyllis M.
THORNTON

SIGNUM

© Copyright 2006, Signum, Inc. Printed in the United States of America. All rights reserved. No part of this book may be reproduced or transmitted in any form or by any means, electronic or mechanical, including photocopying, recording, or by an information storage and retrieval system without permission in writing from the publisher.

Inside Advice on Marketing Senior Housing—The 15 Critical Components of Success is published with a companion CD, the *Marketing Plan Template*. The CD or its contents may not be reproduced or transmitted in any form or by any means, electronic or mechanical, including photocopying, recording, or by an information storage and retrieval system without permission in writing from the publisher.

The author has made every effort to ensure the accuracy and completeness of information contained in this book, and assumes no responsibility for errors, inaccuracies, omissions, or any inconsistency herein. Any slights of people, place, or organization are unintentional.
First printing 2006.

Library of Congress Control Number: 2006901145
ISBN-10: 0-9777938-0-X
ISBN-13: 978-0-9777938-0-8

To my husband Roy,
and
to my father,
Henry G. Watts,
in memoriam.

Contents

Foreword xxiii
Introduction xxv

1

Environmental Scan—Plan With Your Eyes Wide Open 2

The Market Service Area ▪ The Target Market ▪ Demographic and Psychographic Profiles ▪ Consumer Analysis Tools ▪ The Competitive Audit ▪ Strategic and Tactical Competitive Maneuvers ▪ Strengths and Weaknesses ▪ Prospect Objections Versus Occupancy Inpediments ▪ Product, Service, and Price Assessment ▪ Repositioning Prequisites

2

Marketing Objectives And Strategy—Set Your Coordinates 16

The Marketing Audit ▪ The Occupancy Principle ▪ The Sales Objective—Formula and Calculations ▪ Market-Ready Units ▪ Unit Count Recap ▪ Move-In and Attrition Analysis ▪ Information Trending ▪ Lead and Sales Analysis ▪ Qualified Lead Count ▪ Lead and Sales Source Analysis ▪ Referral Versus Paid Advertising Sources ▪ Lead-to-Sale Close Rate ▪ The Lead Objective—Formula and Calculations ▪ Sum up Your Marketing Coordinates ▪ Turning the Numbers into Strategies ▪ Maintenance and Growth Strategies

3

Customer Service—The Core Of Every Marketing Program 32

Customer Service Defined ▪ Customer Service Concepts ▪ Customer Expectations and Perceptions ▪ Training Framework ▪ Telephone Protocols and Training Tips ▪ Physical Plant Appearance ▪ Maintenance, Housekeeping and Cosmetic Décor ▪ Staff Appearance ▪ Management as Role Models ▪ Standards for Professional Dress ▪ Staff Attitudes and Actions ▪ Business Etiquette and Manners ▪ Staff Training Techniques ▪ Marketing's Contribution to Customer Service

4

Marketing And Sales Manpower—How To Staff For Success   42

The Five Essential Marketing Functions ▪ The Team Approach to Marketing ▪ How to Configure the Marketing and Sales Team ▪ Factors That Impede Staff Productivity ▪ Optimum Models for Staff Time Allocation to Marketing and Sales ▪ Productivity and Performance Goals ▪ Staffing Configurations and Capacity ▪ Training and Education ▪ Selecting the Right Training Resources ▪ Training Topics and Modules ▪ Staff Compensation ▪ Base Salary and Commission Programs—Structure and Wages

5

Marketing Information System—The Science Of Decision Making   54

Lead-Management Software ▪ Information Architecture ▪ Demographic Data ▪ Psychographic Data—How to Track Marketing Barriers and Prospect Preferences ▪ Marketing Data—Lead and Sales Sources, Lead Status, Active and Inactive Prospect Codes ▪ Sales Data ▪ Database Management Procedures ▪ Lead-Management Procedures ▪ Software Protocols ▪ Prospect Procedures ▪ The Wait-List ▪ Wait-List Strategies

6

Information Center And Resources—The Ideal Sales Environment   70

What to Call Your Work Area ▪ Single-and Multi-Suite Office Settings ▪ Locations, Furnishings, and Appointments ▪ The Closing Room ▪ Required Resources ▪ The Use of Resident Apartments ▪ Model Apartment Standards and Specifications ▪ How to Show and Sell Apartments ▪ Market-Ready Apartments—Practices and Protocols

7

Strategic Networking—The Kind Of Publicity Money Can't Buy   80

Strategic Networking Defined ▪ Networking in the Scheme of Things ▪ Why Networking Endeavors Stall ▪ How to Work Your Markets From the Inside Out ▪ Primary and Secondary Focus Market Networking Techniques ▪ The Speaker's Bureau ▪ Public Relations as a Sub-Component of Marketing ▪ How to Network With the Press ▪ Roles, Goals, and Performance Standards

Special Events—Programs That Pique Market Interest 92

The Role and Goals of Event Marketing ▪ Educational and Social Program Positioning ▪ Imaginative Themes That Inspire Interest ▪ Topics to Avoid ▪ The Media Mix—PSAs, Direct Mail, Print, and Electronic Media Use ▪ The Special Events Marketing Matrix ▪ How to Match Your Event Programming to Your Marketing Strategy ▪ Advertising Integration and Appeal ▪ The Day of the Show—Event Planning and Preparation Logistics

Creative Design And Copywriting—What To Say And Portray 104

The Challenge of Age-Biased Advertising ▪ Crafting the Right Message—Selling Points and Presentation Formats ▪ Watch Your Language—Words and Phrases to Avoid ▪ How to Describe a Continuum of Care ▪ Graphic Design Visuals and Images—The Problem with Conventional Approaches ▪ How to Cast Your Community ▪ Images That Have Universal Market Appeal ▪ The Lowdown on Branding

Collateral Materials—Print Communications That Pack A Punch 114

The Role and Use of Collateral Materials ▪ The Information Brochure—Design Elements and Specifications ▪ The Role of Information Inserts ▪ Floor Plan, Services and Amenities, Contract Documents, and Price Sheet Design Techniques ▪ Introductory Brochures ▪ The Stationery Package ▪ The Marketing Newsletter—Copy and Layout ▪ The Collateral CD and DVD ▪ Controlling Costs—Do-It-Yourself Design Versus the Use of Outside Agencies

Paid Media—Prerequisites To Advertising Success 128

The Role of Paid Advertising in Your Marketing Program ▪ Test Your Advertising Readiness—Quiz ▪ How Advertising Stacks Up in the Critical Component Line-Up ▪ The Case Against Paid Media—All the Wrong Reasons to Advertise ▪ The Price-to-Value Relationship—The Relative Worth of Direct Mail, Print Media, and Electronic Media

12

Direct Mail—The Right Tool For The Target Market   134

Direct Mail's Multi-Faceted Marketing Benefits ▪ How to Plan Your Direct Mail Campaign ▪ Potential Recipients ▪ The Rented Direct Mail List ▪ What to Send and When ▪ The Direct Mail Marketing Matrix ▪ How to Match Your Direct Mail Campaign to Your Marketing Strategy ▪ How to Increase Your Rate of Return ▪ Optimum Letter Shop, Design, and Flight Times ▪ E-Mail Marketing

13

Print Media—How To Choose It And When To Use It   144

Correlating Print Media Placement to Your Marketing Strategy ▪ Media Classifications—Major Dailies, Neighborhood and Specialty Publications, Directories, and Billboard Advertising ▪ Print Media Frequency and Flights ▪ Design and Copy Specifications ▪ When It's Okay to Advertise More ▪ Assessing the Response Rate ▪ The Print Media Plan

14

Electronic Media—Broadcast Basics To Reach The Masses   152

The Relative Role and Value of Radio, Television, and Web-Based Advertising ▪ PSAs as a Low-Cost and Appropriate Advertising Tool ▪ Determining Whether Electronic Media are Suited to Your Market ▪ Tips for Radio and Television Advertising ▪ Getting Wired for the Web ▪ Designing Your Site

15

Marketing Plan, Time Line, And Budget—Drafting The Document   160

Why You Need a Formal Marketing Plan ▪ The Marketing Plan Template ▪ Goals, Objectives, Strategy, and Tactics ▪ Marketing Time Frames and Time Lines ▪ Gantt Charts ▪ The Marketing Budget—The Right Way to Resource Your Program

Conclusion   169

Index   171

Tables and Figures

Table 1 ■ Unit Count Recap   20

Table 2 ■ Move-In and Attrition Analysis   21

Table 3 ■ Sales Objective   22

Table 4 ■ Lead Count Analysis   23

Table 5 ■ Lead and Sales Source Analysis   25

Table 6 ■ Lead-to-Sale Close Rate   27

Table 7 ■ Lead Objective   28

Table 8 ■ Net Lead Objective   29

Table 9 ■ Staff Performance Goals and Capacity   48

Table 10 ■ Sample Commission Scale   53

Figure 1 ■ Sample Training Session Outline   51

Figure 2 ■ Sample Lead-Management Protocols   65

Figure 3 ■ Special Events Marketing Matrix   98

Figure 4 ■ Direct Mail Marketing Matrix   139

Figure 5 ■ Manpower Gantt Chart   165

Companion CD

The Marketing Plan Template ■ Template Instructions & Action Steps ■ Additional Resources

FOREWORD

Like most industries, senior housing is proceeding through a life cycle. It has moved beyond the introduction and growth stages of product development, and is now entering maturity. Competition is intense, consumer tastes have changed, market saturation has occurred, and consequently, sales have slowed or destabilized.

These trends, however, are not indicative of the last stage of a product's life cycle, irreversible decline. On the contrary, organizations are taking great care to manage their senior housing continuums, and are responding with dynamic plans to extend their service tenure. New senior housing prototypes are being introduced, and existing product is being repositioned and rejuvenated.

Senior housing providers are also sharpening their marketing programs with the intent of becoming more sophisticated and systematic—to tap into the best thinking that's out there. That's why *Inside Advice on Marketing Senior Housing—The 15 Critical Components of Success* is so important. Until now, there's been no single-source schematic for implementing a well thought out, professional marketing program. Author Phyllis Thornton and contibutor Christine Wirthwein, talented and experienced senior housing consultants, have laid down a solid foundation of marketing wisdom that takes the reader through a logical sequence of strategies and tactics, provided in a practical, "how-to" style of instruction.

Inside Advice on Marketing Senior Housing does an excellent job of centering our thinking in a way that removes our inadvertent biases and creative mental blocks. It provides razor sharp focus and valuable content to fill in dangerous gaps in our thinking, while efficiently eliminating unnecessary overlaps. It also includes what most business books don't, an innovative planning tool, on CD, that allows you to take all the important ideas put forth, and customize them to your own situation. Once you've read the entire book, its major elements should be reviewed weekly, like the preflight checklist of an airline pilot. Then, start your day by turning to any one of the "15 Critical Components of Success" for a quick reference and answers to specific marketing issues.

Every now and then, a rare individual comes on the scene and touches the lives of many people with kindness, compassion, talent, and creativity. Phyllis Thornton is one of those rare individuals. Over the past 25 years, she has left her mark of success on hundreds of senior living communities. Her positive impacts have improved staff performance while directly and indirectly touching the lives of thousands of seniors. There are many successful senior living professionals, but very few are willing or able to share their success with others in a no-nonsense, practical manner. Phyllis Thornton has accomplished that objective.

You will find there is much more to *Inside Advice on Marketing Senior Housing* than just strategies, action items, and punch lists. It's a blueprint to the enhanced financial performance of your properties, and the resulting increase in the professional performance of the individuals using this book—and a benefit to the residents they serve.

Inside Advice on Marketing Senior Housing is clearly the right resource at the right time for our industry.

JIM MOORE
Moore Diversified Services, Inc.

Introduction

Long gone are the days when hosting a cheerful open house and producing a pretty brochure passed for a marketing program. Today, maintaining and protecting your market amid fierce competition and rapid-fire industry change requires solving complex issues. It's a time where no one's future is assured. If marketing planning falters, an occupancy goal that looked like a sure thing can suddenly become a pipe dream. If marketing execution is incorrect, full occupancy can turn into vacancies before you know it.

While senior housing has never been a simple business, today it's more complicated than ever before. In fact, you might be tempted to call it something stronger—chaos.

Marketing has suddenly become crucial.

While the senior housing industry has advanced, one aspect of the business has not. Training, educational, and credentialing resources to prepare marketing and sales professionals for changes and challenges have simply not kept pace. Search the Internet, libraries, and bookstores for a comprehensive, industry-custom marketing compendium and you come up empty-handed. Attend conferences and seminars and you get information snippets and consultant sales pitches. Even college-level curricula offer little information that pertains to our specialized profession.

For the most part, education has come about through trial and error; our teacher has been hard-earned experience.

At last there is an answer to your information needs: *Inside Advice on Marketing Senior Housing—The 15 Critical Components of Success*. It teaches you everything you need to know about marketing senior housing. It tells you how to achieve occupancy success. It shows you how to attain marketing mastery. It inspires you to take charge of your marketing destiny. There is no better tool to guide you to marketing success.

You won't find ivory tower theories in the chapters ahead, only practical solutions and proven strategies. Managers, marketers, and sales professionals alike will find *Inside Advice on Marketing Senior Housing* packed with cutting-edge ideas and time-tested techniques. Every detail of planning and implementing a strategic and tactical senior housing marketing program is covered, from the use of market research to position your community to the subtle nuances of creating advertising campaigns that have the greatest market appeal.

Inside Advice on Marketing Senior Housing is more than just a "how-to" book. It's a "how to think about marketing" book. Its genesis began during my career as the owner and President of Signum, Inc., a national industry marketing firm that served organizations spanning the continuum of care. After working with hundreds of communities over 25 years, I began to discern certain marketing patterns. These patterns grew into a body of knowledge that I termed the "critical components of marketing."

My retirement created the time to write this book with the goal of providing a comprehensive educational solution to the information dearth that has hampered the marketing profession since its inception. I invited Christine Wirthwein, President, Wirthwein Corporation Marketing & Advertising, to also contribute her insights. That's why the book is entitled *Inside Advice on Marketing Senior Housing*. Christine and I agreed on a no-holds-barred approach where two consultants "tell all."

Inside Advice on Marketing Senior Housing—The 15 Critical Components of Success is a "plug and play" system that takes the mystery out of marketing. It eliminates guesswork, stalled starts, and floundering progress. It saves you time, money, and energy. It's about smart marketing and how to build a framework that will take you into the future so you don't have to scramble every time there's a dip in occupancy or another project added to your to-do list. A chapter is devoted to each of the 15 critical components, defining what each component is, how it works, how it's applied, and how it integrates with a systematic marketing plan and program.

- Environmental Scan
- Marketing Objectives and Strategy
- Customer Service
- Marketing and Sales Manpower
- Marketing Information System
- Information Center and Resources
- Strategic Networking
- Special Events
- Creative Design and Copywriting
- Collateral Materials
- Paid Media
- Direct Mail
- Print Media
- Electronic Media
- Marketing Plan, Time Line, and Budget

As an added bonus, *Inside Advice on Marketing Senior Housing* comes with a companion CD that contains a *Marketing Plan Template*. The *Template* is designed to help you create your own marketing plan, or to strengthen a program that you already have in place. It's a multi-faceted tool that provides instructions, action steps, and worksheets to draft a marketing plan that you can put to work right away, and create a plan prototype that you can use time and again in the years to come.

Inside Advice on Marketing Senior Housing gives you the insights, information, and tools to achieve occupancy success. It shows you how to create a marketing program that is integrated and all encompassing, that embraces the right strategy, reaches the right people, and evolves in response to marketplace changes.

It's the formula for marketing success, and now it's yours.

PHYLLIS M. THORNTON

> Begin your marketing plan unaware
> of the world around you,
> and you'll be flying blind
> and by the seat of your pants.

1

Environmental Scan—Plan With Your Eyes Wide Open

If you expected to flip open the first chapter of *Inside Advice on Marketing Senior Housing* and read all about advertising advantages and sales strategies, you will have to fast-forward more than a few pages. Those marketing components are covered much later in the book, and later on is exactly where they belong. Right now, it's time for a little homework. Your first assignment is to perform an environmental scan.

If the mere thought of a detailed analysis makes you nod off, then consider this: To succeed, you must understand the rapidly changing environment in which you operate—and then use this intelligence to formulate a marketing plan that navigates the changing terrain. Begin your marketing unaware of the world around you, and you'll be flying blind and by the seat of your pants.

When an environmental scan is performed for an entire organization, it's referred to as a SWOT analysis—a study of strengths, weaknesses, opportunities, and threats.

The environmental scan is an extension of an operational SWOT, except it is framed in a marketing context. Think of this first critical marketing component as a research tool that provides a snapshot of your local market, your target market, your competition, and how well your organization is serving your market through its products and services. Insights from this study enable you to create a program to leverage marketing-related strengths, capitalize on opportunities, rectify weaknesses, and thwart threats. Let's disconnect from the academics of organizational management and get down to the brass tacks of planning with your eyes wide open. Effective marketing planning requires a strategic mind-set. You're seeking answers to four basic questions:

- Where is your market?
- Who is your market and what do they want?
- Who is serving your market?
- How well is your organization serving your market?

The Market Area—Mark Your Territory

A market service area (or market area) is the geographic region from which you derive the majority of your residents. Knowing the exact geography of your market service area is important, for the idea is to patrol and protect your borders while you market to the inhabitants within them.

The general rule of thumb is that approximately 70 to 80 percent of your residents will originate from a particular geography. While this area is visually definitive, it's not a perfect circle that surrounds your site. It's usually an odd shaped footprint whose size is influenced by many elements. Foremost is a factor known as "neighborhood affiliation." Older adults want to remain close to home and near family, religious, recreational, and healthcare connections. If your community location is considered to be "in the neighborhood," you can count on that neighborhood being in your market service area.

Topographical boundaries, such as rivers, mountains, and major highways; city, county, and state lines; and area economics and ethnicity also define your operational borders. However, these elements take a backseat to one factor that can shrink your domain: predatory competition. A new competitive player who sets up shop in your backyard can transform the terrain overnight. Your market area just got smaller because the consumer-rich geography that you once laid claim to is now being gobbled up by the new guy on the block.

Before you can protect your market service area, you first have to define it. This is easily done by determining where your residents resided before they moved to your community. While zip code data is the most common geography of study, you can also define your market service area by a mileage range or by county. For example, a community that is located in a densely populated area may draw residents who live just a few miles instead of several zip codes away. Conversely, a rural-based community may serve residents throughout an entire county.

The *Marketing Plan Template* provides instructions and a Geographic Origin Analysis table to help you ascertain and analyze your market service area. As you work through your assessment, be careful not to falsely inflate the size of your market service area by including geography that only contributes a small percentage of your resident population—for example, those from which you've had only two or three move-ins. Remember that for every additional zip code, mile, or county that you include in the defined market area, the aggregate count of senior adult households rises. The key for inclusion is whether a significant number of households located in a particular area (zip code, mileage range, or county) will move to your location or opt for a closer alternative.

So you've assembled the data and you can state with authority that you know the geography of your market service area. Now what? Here's where you translate dry data to actionable marketing information.

The immediate and obvious application of this data is in marketing planning. Your market service area is the bull's-eye for your outreach and advertising efforts, and the upcoming chapters will discuss the multiple tactics used to target this important geography.

As you update your market service area data each year, you're also able to spot important patterns, particularly if contributing zip codes have changed. Perhaps your analysis surfaced a small but growing number of individuals originating from a new and previously untapped zip code or neighborhood. This seemingly obscure finding represents a gold nugget, and you'll want to mine for more gold where those sales came from.

Or you may find that your market area is shrinking in size. This is a sure symptom that something is amiss. This something is usually new competition. Today, many providers find themselves hemmed in by competitors. Let this trend go unchecked and you'll find yourself on the drought side of adequate market supply.

There is one final point to make before we move on. No matter how hard you try, marketing strategies—and specifically advertising—cannot artificially expand an established market area; they will not induce folks who do not identify with your area to migrate to your area. You can spend yourself broke trying to reach senior consumers in distant lands—and in the end, they'll opt to remain in the

> Marketing strategies, and specifically advertising, cannot artificially expand an established market area.

neighborhood that they know so well. It is possible, however, to increase your reach and penetration within your market service area. You'll learn how to bolster your backyard marketing efforts in the chapters to come.

The Target Market—Find Your Customer

Your market service area is all about territory; your target market is all about the senior adults located within your territory. To secure sales and sustain occupancy, you have to define who those individuals are and what they want.

On the surface, the senior housing market seems obvious—it's senior consumers, right? Well, sort of. In the early years of retirement housing development, we stampeded to respond to the growing mature market. During this building fervor, providers failed to "target" the market—to precisely define who they were and what they wanted. Whether because we thought we knew it all or because we didn't know enough, we erroneously assumed the senior adult population was one big, healthy, homogeneous group.

The industry believed that all senior adults wanted the same exact "congregate" housing and just couldn't wait to congregate at our new communities. Project unit types and sizes were designed to maximize density, not satisfy consumer desires. Pricing structures were based on the profit we needed, not what the consumer was willing to pay. Service packages were loaded up to justify our high prices or pegged to what we thought a senior consumer required, rather than what they might desire.

Because proper research about the target market is seldom performed before a community is developed, the product may not be the best fit with the marketplace. Marketing is then expected to sell product that isn't all that marketable. It's no wonder that so many communities today have chronic vacancies.

The purpose of this history lesson is to demonstrate that the penalty for entering the market, without knowing your market, is that you will eventually have to compensate for ill-conceived product through intensive and expensive marketing.

The Demographic Profile—Stack Up the Statistics

It's your job to make sure that your product and marketing program are designed with the needs and desires of your target market in mind. Here's how.

The first step in defining your target market is to determine its demographic profile. "Demographics" are measurable population characteristics such as age, income, gender, marital status, and ethnicity.

> "Demographics" are measurable population characteristics such as age, income, gender, marital status, and ethnicity.

Identifying your target market demographic profile isn't all that hard because it's right in front of you: It's a mirror image of your current market—your existing residents. You need to know their vital statistics so you can seek and find more of the same.

Age is the first target market demographic to define and it's determined by the average age of residents when they enter your community, not the age of your current residents or the age you wish they would be when they enter.

Next, set your income target. Like age, base this figure on the financial profile of your residents.

You can also describe the gender, marital status, ethnic, and religious affiliation characteristics of your market. However, the primary profile should define the target market's age and income, as reflected in your residency profiles and as indicated by your organization's residency criteria. For example: "The target market is all individuals aged 75 or older with incomes of $35,000 or more per year who reside in a market service area comprised of five zip codes (list zip codes)."

> The presence of an aged population makes it tough to attract a younger crowd that isn't interested in looking at the future that awaits them.

This demographic silhouette is all you need to accomplish some sleek and sophisticated marketing. For example, data is available from market research and mail list vendors on how many individuals in your market service area meet your target market profile and where they are in geographic location. With this information you can reach right in and tap your target market on the shoulder with high-impact direct mail marketing. Understanding your target market demographic profile puts the science into your advertising strategies, a concept we'll cover more in Chapter 12, Direct Mail.

Some of you may be throwing up your hands in protest saying you don't want more of the "same kind" of residents. You want that active, on-the-go, 60-something-year-old, not the 80-something-year-old that now calls your community home. The ever-growing presence of an aged population makes it tough to attract a younger crowd that isn't interested in looking every day at the future that awaits them.

However, you can no more manipulate resident profiles (and your target market profile) through marketing than you can artificially alter your market service area. Some communities devote a lot of advertising dollars to attracting a younger age group. It doesn't pay off and here's why: If your community offers primarily studio and small one-bedroom apartments, with a service package of two or three meals a day, weekly housekeeping, and access to assisted living or long-term care, it is unlikely that you will draw the 60-something market in a big way. However, you will attract the older (and often more frail) individual who is willing to settle for less living space just to have access to support services now and in the future.

A stringent prescreening process that discriminates for the "ideal" resident profile isn't the fix either. This triage only results in vacant units because the residency criteria do not match the profile of the individual your community is likely to attract.

Unless your organization is willing to reposition its unit mix and services to appeal to younger consumers, you have to face facts. Embrace the business that you're in—instead of trying to change it by manipulating marketing and residency requirements. Likewise, off-target advertising that portrays fantasy resident profiles will yield nothing more than phantom results; you have to market, and accurately portray, what you have to work with.

The Psychographic Profile—Listen and Learn

The market area and target market demographic assessment just outlined provides solid information about where your market is, and who it is in age and income. Now we come to the last aspect of what target marketing success is all about: your ability to ask, listen, and respond to what the market wants. What are your target market's opinions about senior housing? What do they want in accommodations and services? What are they willing to pay? And the million-dollar question: Are they willing to move into your community? Without this information, you're back to flying blind. The only way to determine what customers want is to ask and listen.

> With psychographic analysis, you are gathering data that funnels into the decision-making process of how to best position your community to fit dominant market characteristics.

Obtaining and analyzing information on your target market's mind-set is known as psychographic analysis. This fancy phrase suggests there is more going on here than jotting down notes about a prospect's interests or concerns. With psychographic analysis, you are gathering and measuring a multitude of data that funnels into the decision-making process of how to best position your community and marketing program to fit dominant target market characteristics.

For example, what are the foremost unit types of interest (studio, one-, two-, or three-bedroom apartments)? Does the market prefer apartments or a detached dwelling, such as a patio home? What services do customers need and desire and how should these services be packaged (all-inclusive or à la carte)? What is the preferred healthcare service delivery model—is it simply health and wellness programming or do customers want access to a full continuum of care?

You can find out what your market wants using various consumer-analysis tools. These include:

Mail or Phone Surveys. These are the real muscle of consumer survey research because the measurement of market profiles and preferences occurs on a large scale, with sample sizes in the range of 300 to 600 target market households. This degree of research is particularly indicated for a contemplated new development because it provides a blueprint of product, service, and pricing models that has the most market appeal. Because of their complexity, mail and phone surveys are administered by, or with the assistance of, a market research firm and with (or following) a market feasibility study.

Focus Group Surveys. These surveys assess the attitudes and preferences of your resident population and/or your prospects. They can be a casual affair, administered by you and your team, or they can be a formal process facilitated by a market research firm. Regardless of the venue, be cautious in how you apply the survey results. Because focus groups are composed of only 10 to 15 individuals, the information you gather should not be your sole source of intelligence in designing new projects or programs. Always test your focus group results with a comprehensive research instrument such as a mail or phone survey.

Resident Surveys. While the intent of a resident survey is to measure satisfaction, it can be augmented to address your marketing information needs. By asking a few more questions, you can determine the reasons that led residents to your community. For example, you might ask residents how important were your location, reputation, service offerings, and pricing in their selection process. What problems were residents trying to solve by moving to your community? What lifestyle changes were they seeking? Many of us assume that it's the intangibles of "security," "peace of mind," and "companionship" that lead consumers to our door. However, what about the headaches, hassles, and expense of home upkeep? Find out what other communities residents investigated and why they selected you in the end. What you learn will help you identify your marketing messages and selling points.

Resident surveys are especially valuable if you have a population comprised of a particular affinity group (such as religious or fraternal organizations). It's a great way (and about the only way) to assess their profiles and preferences.

Marketing Information System (MKIS). A properly designed information system is a powerful consumer survey research tool. Using enhanced lead-management software as the data collection tool, an MKIS creates a database of target market profiles and preferences based on information acquired by the sales team as they talk with their prospects. This data is used to assess and direct the marketing program's performance. The architecture and applications of this critical marketing component are covered in Chapter 5, Marketing Information System.

These consumer-analysis options are identified for your information—they should not be construed as absolute research assignments. The tool you use to assess target market preferences must be matched to the job at hand. New project due diligence mandates the full research gauntlet. For the immediate assignment of marketing planning, you can rely on common sense supported by a solid marketing information system. After all, the marketing and sales teams are on the frontlines every day talking to an endless number of consumers. That information, aggregated into an MKIS, reveals everything you need to know about your target market profile.

Let's change the pace a bit and do some fieldwork. It's time to check out the competition.

The Competition Shake Down

Since the environmental scan is about the external market, you're obligated to take note of the competition. However, the point of researching the competition is to learn from it, not to mimic it. "Chase the customer, not the competition" is good advice often unheeded by the industry. Your community must be designed with the consumer in mind—not based on what the competition is doing.

> There are two forms of competition: mind-share and market-share.

Competition takes two forms: mind-share and market-share. Mind-share competition occurs when providers compete for the market's attention. In these situations, multiple established providers are trying to outgun each other by using extensive advertising.

If you're asleep at the wheel, mind-share competition can advance to market-share competition—when providers compete for, and win, the market's business.

Confusion about the difference between mind-share and market-share competition often leads to unnecessary hand-wringing and subsequently a confused and diffused marketing effort. You need to pay attention to all area providers. However, it's your market-share competitors that pose a direct, measurable threat. A market-share competitor is:

- A community that draws its residents from the same market service area as you. Don't worry too much about the retirement community that is located on the other side of town; you want to know who is siphoning residents from your market service area.

- A community to whom you lose leads or sales in significant numbers. Two or three lost sales a year is nothing to get nervous about, but if the numbers creep higher, you definitely want to stop the competitor's encroachment into your camp.

After you identify your market-share competition, it's time to embark on a reconnaissance mission. You need to perform a competitive audit. Compiling a cursory list of the competitions' pricing or establishing cozy cross-referral and networking relationships with your marketing contemporaries doesn't begin to scratch the surface. A comprehensive competitive audit goes much further—in both how often it is performed and the data you collect.

Assess the competition quarterly, using a combination of telephone and on-site interviews to collect pertinent information. Baseline intelligence gathering includes attributes such as physical plant characteristics, unit mix, amenities, services, care levels, financial program(s) and fees. The Competitive Provider Profile in the *Marketing Plan Template* will guide you in capturing these and other important provider characteristics.

After you have established a profile on each community, the competitive audit process becomes more abbreviated; you only have to scan for offering updates. However, don't be lulled into the task of filling out forms and forget about the goal of the assignment. Remember, you're not studying the competition to determine what your community should offer. The correct application of competitive data is to assemble it into "actionable information" that is used at a strategic and tactical level.

Strategic Maneuvers and Tactical Trench Work

If you're experiencing chronic vacancies, you should compare competitor occupancy rates to your own. If all providers have vacant units, then the issue may be too little market for too many units. However, if other market area providers enjoy higher occupancy, find out why. Is it due to a superior marketing program or a superior product?

Or suppose your community has a lot of studio units or small one-bedroom apartments and your vacancies are concentrated in these units. The immediate assumption would be that these units are not marketable and need to be converted to more spacious one- and two-bedroom apartments. Stop right there. Look before you leap into any product repositioning. If the competition has the same or similar unit types, are their smaller units sitting empty as well? If not, why not? What are they doing or offering that can account for their occupancy success?

Your overall assessment may well reveal that the sheer number of market area units has increased over the last several years, and this product proliferation has affected your occupancy. You're not alone—few remaining markets, if any, still have low levels of competition. So if you can't hold back the tide, what do you do?

First, avoid being passive and paralyzed by a fatalistic attitude. Instead, be assertive. You have to fight for your fair market-share—that's what marketing is all about. Increased competition mandates more aggressive marketing. In a "saturated market" (too much product), your sales and occupancy must be achieved at the competition's expense.

> In a saturated market, your occupancy must be achieved at the competition's expense.

Another way to protect and expand your market-share is to capitalize on your competition's weaknesses. What do you offer that tops the competition in mission, experience, unit types and sizes, amenities, services, pricing, and marketing and sales?

Obtain and review your competition's collateral materials and contract documents. Read the fine print for product and pricing nuances that may not be all that appealing to the market. Make sure you or someone you know is on the competition's mailing list so you can stay abreast of their activities. Watch the newspapers and set up a clipping file of competitive print ads. Do some detective work with the aid of a mystery shopper to obtain insights into a competitor's "point of contact" service quality. You may feel threatened by the new community that just opened down the road, but you can sharpen your marketing edge by remembering (and adhering to) this marketing adage: There are no superior communities, only superior staff. For example, if your new competitor greets incoming callers using a cold and confusing voice mail system, you'll want to capitalize on this weakness and make sure you have a warm and lively receptionist answering your phone. This example is just one of many ways to work your competitive findings into smart marketing communications that send customers your way and into memorable service quality that keeps customers coming your way.

Strengths and Weaknesses

The information you've gathered so far sets the stage for the final segment of the environmental scan where it all comes together. It's now time to turn your attention inward to answer the last question: How well is your organization serving your market?

You don't need to perform a full-blown organizational SWOT to find the answer. Rather, your internal assessment is a slice of the SWOT to isolate those strengths and weaknesses that impact marketing. The twofold purpose of this evaluation is to: 1) design tactics that capitalize upon your strengths and minimize your weaknesses, and 2) team up with management to tackle the occupancy impediments that are beyond marketing's control and capacity to correct.

Begin your assessment with the easiest aspect of the process: identifying your strengths. Center your thoughts on the customer and think about those attributes and offerings that your prospects find most appealing. Seek out strengths in everything from the organization's history and mission to the particulars of product and price. Avoid cliché characteristics such as "good reputation" or "quality care and service," and strive to identify strengths of substance that clearly separate your community from the competition, also known as the "Unique Selling Proposition" or USP. The USP is used repeatedly in your marketing and sales messages.

The next step is to identify your "marketing barriers"—those facility characteristics that hamper lead generation, sales, or occupancy.

> A marketing barrier is any characteristic that hampers lead generation, sales, or occupancy.

If you're one of the fortunate communities that is barrier free, then you can skip the obstacle audit. You simply need to summarize your strengths and then move on in the book to learn how to better market your already superior offerings. However, if you're faced with product, service, or price-related barriers, then you'll need to document what they are.

When identifying and working through your marketing barriers, be judicious. You are collecting this information with the intent of changing or reshaping your marketing program or even the services you offer. This process is more than just creating a hit list of prospects' objections; it's a serious endeavor to document obstacles to occupancy. First, you're not going to run down every little rabbit hole looking for every little marketing limitation. You're going to compartmentalize your barrier assessment into three areas: product (physical plant, apartments, and amenities), service, and price. Second, you can't be all things to all people so you need to isolate the big issues that block your sales progress. And finally, you'll need to determine the cause for the barrier. Who knows, the problem may have nothing to do with product limitations, but more to do with you and how you're marketing the product.

Product, Service, and Price Assessment

Take a product, service, and price tour to scrutinize your community from the "customer's point-of-view."

Does your community have excellent curb appeal, from well-manicured grounds to professional and attractive signage? Step inside and consider everything, from the building's architectural design to the cosmetic décor. Is what you see superior or subpar?

While we go the distance to sell the intangibles of "security" and "peace of mind," the customer eventually gravitates toward tangible benefits. Consider your target market preferences and compare this profile to your product. Take into account unit mix (number of studio, one- two-, and three-bedroom units), size and design, appointments, appliances, fixtures, and the overall fit and finish quality. Also assess the ergonomics, environmental design, and décor of those areas that serve as extensions to the residents' apartments, from hallways to lobbies to amenities areas.

Now think about the type and intensity of services offered in relation to price. Review the services included in the monthly fee and what services are available at an additional charge. Are the services you provide and the way they are priced and packaged a good fit with your target market preferences?

Your financial program is the last area to assess. You'll need to consider both your financial positioning (e.g., entry fee, rental, or ownership) and price points (the fees associated with each unit type). With most consumers, the decision-making process begins and ends in their wallet, so if your community is beyond the customer's economic reach or their financial comfort zone, all other offerings become a moot point.

Prospect Objections Versus Occupancy Impediments

Since you're deliberately looking for limitations, be prepared to surface at least a few, and perhaps a lot, of marketing obstacles. The most common include units that are just too small for the market's taste or whose views (of rooflines or mechanicals) are not what consumers had in mind, or apartment locations that require traveling the length of a football field to access certain amenity areas. Prospects never want every single service that's included in the monthly fee, which by the way is "just too expensive."

Here is where you need to slow down and assess the facts. Countless communities have repositioned their unit mix, expanded their apartment sizes, modified their services, and even altered their financial programs only to find that these changes did not result in an appreciable increase in sales. Why? Because the problem they were trying to correct was not legitimate, or that big to begin with. The extent of the problem was based on information from a few individuals who seem to find never-ending excuses to defer moving to a retirement community.

So before you can state that a particular issue constitutes a bona fide marketing barrier, you need to quantify the extent to which the supposed barrier affects sales. Are there several dozen or several hundred prospects who express concern over a particular issue? Moreover, how many more prospects would move in if you corrected or removed the barrier? The latter is the real litmus test of a marketing barrier.

Another reason repositioning strategies don't always net new sales is that barrier symptoms are often incorrectly diagnosed and staff treat the "perceived" problem versus the "real" problem. Take the pricing barrier as an example.

A real price barrier is when the product is priced beyond a community's target market.

A perceived price barrier is when the product is correctly price-aligned with the market and the market can afford the product, but the market "thinks" the product is too expensive in relation to the value offered, to what the market prefers to spend, or to other housing alternatives.

If you're concerned that your financial positioning is all wrong, ask yourself the following questions before you propose a program change:

- Are your price points too high in relation to the value offered or the economic profile of the market (a product-positioning issue)?
- Do prospects not fully understand your offerings (a marketing issue)?
- Is the sales team unable to overcome common prospect objections (a sales issue)?

Making these distinctions is important because the answer points you to the corrective action.

If it's a matter of price alignment with the services offered or the market's economic profile, then marketing and management need to team up to develop a plan for service or price repositioning. If the barrier is due to inadequate consumer education or a weak sales effort, then it's time to ratchet up your marketing program and sales staff training.

Repositioning Prerequisites

The most prudent approach to remedying a barrier is this: Before you change your community offerings in any way, first change the way you market your community. As an extension of this fundamental principle, you should seek to remove barriers by fixing (improving) your services before you fix your building.

For instance, if the appearance of your community isn't all that great, what is the reason for its subpar state? Is it because of dated and shabby furnishings or poor housekeeping and maintenance? Before you spend big bucks on new interiors, why not make the most of what you have through good housekeeping and high maintenance standards that pay attention to the details?

> Before you change your community offerings, first change the way you market your community.

Or let's say you have the seldom used exercise room that's furnished with the standard cast-off exercise equipment. Before you build a multimillion-dollar, state-of-the-art wellness center, why not investigate ways to rejuvenate this amenity with fresh paint, warm lighting, and a thoughtful wellness program that comes complete with a fitness trainer?

Sometimes success is not about changing the business we are in, but in changing the way we do business—doing more of the same, but doing it better.

In some cases however, product repositioning is inevitable. Let's say you have exhausted all avenues to optimize your occupancy as you're presently designed, and you're still experiencing chronic vacancies because of product limitations. Now what? You need to move forward with a plan to either reposition or rebuild what you have. In fact, many organizations are master planning to: 1) correct the problems of their current product, 2) expand their product and services to reach more of the market, and 3) prepare for the next wave of senior consumers: the silent and baby boomer generations.

If your organization has plans to reposition or expand, it's imperative that you verify the market need for this mission and vision with in-depth and impartial demographic and psychographic analysis. There are multiple research tools that will give you the market-driven facts to determine how to best position your organization now and in the years to come. Never modify your unit mix, service package, or financial program without this analysis.

The marketing and sales team should also have a formal voice in the master planning process and a seat at the meetings where the project design and development takes place. After all, it's your department that has the inside track on what senior consumers want and the master plan can benefit from your insights. It's also your department that's ultimately responsible for the master plan's marketing success; you need to know what's ahead in order to ramp up your program accordingly.

We've come to the end of the environmental scan. You know where and who your market is, what they want, and how you stack up. Let's move ahead to the second critical marketing component: how to establish your lead and sales objectives and set your strategic marketing course.

> To be a marketing heavyweight, you need solid skills in arithmetic and problem solving, plus a good dose of common sense.

2

Marketing Objectives And Strategy—Set Your Coordinates

This chapter reveals the formula for obtaining your occupancy goal. Here you will learn how to calculate the marketing plan's lead and sales objectives. You'll also be introduced to marketing strategies that define how aggressive your program needs to be to achieve those objectives. The plan's objectives and strategy are the axis of your marketing program—its coordinates, so to speak. A coordinate is a set of numbers that together describe the exact position of a target. Your target is full occupancy.

Heads up—this critical marketing component is full of valuable planning information and much of it is communicated in math. If you want to be a strategic-minded marketer, you need solid skills in arithmetic and problem solving along with a good dose of common sense. It's the science of marketing, not the art, that separates the marketing heavyweights from the lightweights. Let's be honest: Any thinking individual can provide a prospect tour or paste together a print ad. But do these intermittent and elementary activities influence your occupancy? The answer is no, they don't.

Smart marketing is about asking and obtaining the answers to fundamental objective-setting and planning questions and then using that information to chart your plan's course. Your quest for answers involves delving into all the elements that drive your occupancy: move-ins and attrition, quantity and quality of leads and sales, sources of leads and sales, and your close rate. If you're not clear on the meaning of these terms, sit tight, you will be in a moment. Marketing consultants often refer to this assessment as a "marketing audit." The audit analyzes all the forces and factors that make your marketing world go-round. Without this information, you end up with marketing happenstance, not calculated circumstance. If you're not sold on the idea of another analysis, consider these benefits. A marketing audit:

Renders the figures you need to formulate quantifiable objectives. A true and correct objective isn't stated in subjective terms like "increase occupancy" or "build market awareness." An objective is a measurable action path—complete with numbers.

Shapes the intensity and direction of your marketing plan and program. What is your occupancy goal? Is your current marketing program generating enough leads and sales to achieve that goal? If not, how many more leads and sales does the program need? The answers to these questions dictate the marketing program's aggressiveness. You'll have the facts to work up the best blend of staffing, networking, and advertising tactics to reach your target market and to achieve your target occupancy.

Makes it easy to ascertain if your program is off-track, where it's off-track, and how to put it back on track. For example, are you making the most of your current leads or are they going by the wayside because of poor sales practices? Are your advertising efforts reaching the right places and speaking to the right people? If you're seeking more sales, do you need to accelerate your advertising efforts to build your lead base, or increase your close rate and nail a greater percentage of your present leads?

Translates move-in, attrition, lead, and sales data into actionable information. When you perform a marketing audit you're "data mining"—a fancy phrase for toiling over figures to extract hidden facts. These facts are used to set your objectives and for big-picture program trending and troubleshooting.

The Occupancy Principle

Marketing can seem like a complex maze, but you can eliminate its mystery with the use of some simple math that is founded on one guiding principle:

The Occupancy Principle

Leads generate sales,

Sales generate move-ins,

Move-ins (minus attrition) result in occupancy

These are the essential ingredients of occupancy. Leads generate sales. Sales translate into move-ins. Your move-ins, less resident attrition, determine ending occupancy. Marketing functions as the "flow control." Your program, if properly planned and executed, creates the flow of leads—the lead objective—that will be converted into move-ins—the sales objective.

Let's take a research road trip to show you the route for calculating the plan's lead and sales objectives. You'll also have an opportunity for a few data excursions if you're inclined to take in more of the terrain. As you work through the chapter, be sure to refer to the *Marketing Plan Template*'s action steps and tables to help you map out and summarize your findings.

The Sales Objective

We'll start with the sales objective, because the number of new sales the marketing program must secure dictates the number of leads (lead objective) you need to achieve the sales target.

The sales objective is the number of sales the program must obtain in a 12-month period—the standard duration of a marketing plan. It's the sum of two variables: vacant units and anticipated attrition.

> Sales Objective = Vacant Units + Attrition

Let's review each component more closely so that you're clear on what to calculate.

The Vagaries of Vacant Units

The first figure to factor into your sales objective is your vacant unit count. This may seem like an obvious number, but staff opinions can vary on what constitutes available inventory. Management tends to report and base their operating budget on the community's total unit count. The problem with this accounting is that it generally includes units that are being used for alternate (and non-revenue-producing) purposes, such as apartments that serve as storage or office space, or are under renovation or construction. Marketing staff, on the other hand, generally consider the community's unit count (and any vacancies) to be only those apartments that are available to show and sell—apartments that are "market-ready."

To identify the vacant unit count that you will use to calculate your sales objective, use the Unit Count Recap table in the *Marketing Plan Template* to first sort your inventory by the total number of units in your community, and

Community A
Table 1 Unit Count Recap

Units	Count	Percent
Total Community Units	175	--
Total Market-Ready Units	171	--
Occupancy Goal [1]	171	100%
Current Occupied Units [1]	163	95%
Vacant Units [1]	**8**	**5%**

(1) Based on Market-Ready Unit Count

then by the total number of units that are market-ready. As illustrated in Community A's Unit Count Recap (Table 1), the next line items are clear-cut ledger entries: the occupancy goal (based on the market-ready unit count), the current number of occupied units, and the variance, which is the number of net (marketable) vacancies.

If your community is expanding, be sure the recap includes any planned units that will need to be presold or that will come on line in the next 12 months. Note these units as a separate line item to distinguish them from your existing inventory. Later in the plan, you'll need to identify the additional resources required to market these units.

Although you've tallied your inventory, you're not done with the subject of market-ready units versus total community units just yet. You need to work with management to make sure your community is maximizing its entire inventory. We'll tell you how in Chapter 6.

The Anomalies of Attrition

Attrition represents the second part of the sales objective equation. Projecting attrition is important because those eventual vacancies will need to be sold as well. To achieve your occupancy goal, the marketing program must produce enough sales and move-ins to fill your vacant units and offset attrition.

Projected attrition can be an average of what your community has experienced over the last three to five years, the prior year, or a variation thereof, given your understanding of your current resident profile. If you don't know these statistics, then you'll need to gather at least three years of historical move-in and attrition data. This summary isn't difficult to assimilate if you use your occupancy reports along with the *Marketing Plan Template*'s Move-In and Attrition Analysis table.

Although it's tempting to take a shortcut, don't make the mistake of collecting too little data. Last year's numbers alone, or even two year's worth of data, will not paint a complete picture. Move-ins and attrition fluctuate and occur in cycles. For example, a recent spike in attrition may be more than a small blip on your occupancy radar—it may be symptomatic of an overall decline that began some time ago. If you input a too-low attrition figure, you run the risk of underestimating your sales objective and pursuing the wrong marketing strategy.

Information Trending

Accounting for the "ins and outs" of your occupancy is more than just a test of your math skills. Look closely and you'll find that the data is infused with trending information. Here's our first research side trip and it's geared toward communities that chronically operate below their budgeted occupancy goal. For such communities, trend analysis is mandatory.

Look at the move-in and attrition data compiled for Community A (Table 2). Over a three-year period, it went from near-full occupancy to below goal occupancy. The staff attributed the occupancy decline to a slowdown in sales. However, this wasn't the case, evidenced by the increase in move-ins that occurred every year. The real cause for Community A's occupancy decline was increasing attrition and a sales velocity that was simply insufficient to counterbalance the escalating outflow.

Community A's findings are a crystal-clear illustration of how move-in and attrition data can help to identify the cause and corrective action for occupancy-distressed communities. They also exemplify a pervasive industry trend: accelerating attrition due to the increasing frailties of incoming residents, compounded by residents who are aging-in-place.

These trends are not likely to change, yet many communities have not supplemented their marketing programs to compensate for their increasing losses. Mounting attrition doesn't mean that you have to revamp your marketing program; you just need to increase its intensity and step-up your sales production. You don't wait for attrition to occur—you assume that it will occur and plan accordingly.

COMMUNITY A

Table 2 Move-In and Attrition Analysis

Move-In and Attrition Summary	Years in Review		
	Prior Year	Year 2	Year 3
Beginning Occupancy	168	173	174
Move-Ins	32	30	26
Attrition	-37	-35	-27
Year-End Actual Occupancy	**163**	**168**	**173**
Year-End Budgeted Occupancy[1]	**175**	**175**	**175**

(1) Does not discriminate for market-ready units

Remember, the marketing program must generate enough move-ins to fill your vacant units and compensate for attrition. The question is how much attrition should you anticipate in your planning? That's where information trending comes in—you use your historical attrition statistics to forecast future attrition activity. Let's say you're the marketing director of Community A. Look again at the three-year data in Table 2. It portends that you should expect to lose at least 30 residents in the coming year.

Filling In the Sales Formula

Now you have all the facts to finalize your sales objective. We'll use Community A's data (Table 3) to summarize the steps and ending output.

COMMUNITY A
Table 3 Sales Objective

Units	Count
Total Community Units	175
Total Market-Ready Units	171
Occupancy Goal	171
Current Occupied Units	163
Vacant Units	8
Projected Attrition	33
Sales Objective	41

Community A has 8 vacant units. Attrition is projected at 33 residents, an average of the prior three-year activity. To achieve the budgeted occupancy goal, the marketing staff must secure 41 sales over the next 12 months (8 vacant units + 33 attrition units = 41 sales).

The Lead Objective

The lead objective is a projection of how many leads your program needs in order to secure the sales target. You calculate the lead objective by dividing the sales objective by a projected close rate. Here's the formula:

$$\text{Lead Objective} = \frac{\text{Sales Objective}}{\text{Close Rate (\%)}}$$

You already know your sales objective, so all you need to do to complete the lead objective equation is to identify the close rate. However, before we work through the close rate calculations and lead objective projection, let's examine the leads you already have on hand. After all, marketing is about more than lead generation—it's about cultivating leads composed of individuals who are likely to move to your community. It's about allocating resources to promotional venues that are proven sources for leads and sales. And finally, it's about converting your leads into commitments through expert sales practices.

Here comes the science again. With a little arithmetic and some time spent studying your marketing landscape, you have the factual framework to control both the sum and substance of your leads and sales: lead quantity and quality, lead and sales sources, and the close rate.

For those of you who use industry-customized lead-management software, analyzing your leads in the manner that we're going to describe is a matter of running a few standard reports. The Lead Count Analysis and the Lead and Sales Source Analysis tables in the *Marketing Plan Template* provide additional data collection formats.

If you track your leads and sales activity manually, or do not compile requisite planning data, you'll likely be unable to perform a meaningful analysis. View the following assessment steps as a model for the comprehensive data that your marketing program must capture in the future. We show you the nuts and bolts of a lead and sales tracking system in Chapter 5.

Lead Count

Begin your assessment with the foremost information item that most marketers are tenacious in tracking—the lead count. Follow the example in Table 4 and use the *Template's* Lead Count Analysis table to record the number of total and qualified leads you have on record.

The total lead count is the sum of all the individuals who have contacted your organization to date (or over the history of the marketing program). Your community may use a different term, such as "prospect," "referral," "inquirer," or "contact," to describe this group. Use whatever phrase you like, just be sure you and your team are clear on its meaning.

COMMUNITY A

Table 4 Lead Count Analysis

Leads	Count	Percent
Total Leads	1,935	--
Qualified Leads	1,300	67%

The qualified lead count is a derivative of your total leads and represents the number of age-, income-, and medically qualified individuals on record. It is the substance of your lead base. The qualified lead base is also known as the "working lead base," the "active lead base," or the "prospect base."

Your data table should resemble that of Community A. It has a total of 1,935 leads on record, of which 1,300 (67%) are qualified leads (Table 4).

Lead and Sales Source

Now segment your qualified leads, and your sales, by lead source. Use prior year, year-to-date, or program-to-date data. This assessment is especially indicated for a community that is using direct mail, print media, or electronic media. When, where, and how much paid media to use is always a conundrum. The answers to these planning questions are found in your lead and sales profiles. You want to repeat successful campaign elements and eliminate the waste, or those vehicles that show low-to-no results as measured in leads and sales.

Even occupancy-stable communities that don't advertise extensively, because of a steady stream of word of mouth referrals, benefit from a lead and sales source analysis. There's a world of individuals and organizations that refer candidates to your community, from residents to local realtors. Understanding which entities and individuals are sending the most referrals your way helps you better direct your outreach efforts.

The *Template's* Lead and Sales Source Analysis instructions and table, along with the example provided for Community A (Table 5), will guide you in sorting your data by the number and percentage of leads and sales attributed to each source.

Notice that Community A's leads and sales database has also been classified by "referral-based sources" and "paid sources." This distinction is important.

Referral-based lead and sales sources constitute word of mouth referrals that originate from residents, friends, family, and staff. This category also includes leads that result from your networking endeavors. Referral-based leads and sales are the ideal because they generally cost less to procure. They are also preconditioned to close in a shorter time frame compared to leads and sales generated by paid advertising.

Paid lead and sales sources represent all the traditional promotional tools: direct mail, print media, and electronic media. Special events marketing can be classed as either a referral-based or a paid lead and sales source. A special event, in and of itself, falls more into the realm of grass roots (referral-based) marketing. However, the use of direct mail and print media to promote event attendance pushes its classification into the paid advertising category.

Leads and sales sourced to paid media come at a higher cost and demonstrate a lower close rate, compared to referral-based sources.

COMMUNITY A
Table 5 Lead and Sales Source Analysis

Lead Source Category	Qualified Leads[1] Count	Qualified Leads[1] Percent	Sales[2] Count	Sales[2] Percent
Referral-Based Sources				
Word of Mouth	580	50%	17	53%
Networking	145	13%	4	13%
Subtotal Referral-Based	725	63%	21	66%
Paid Sources				
Special Events	102	9%	3	9%
Direct Mail	221	19%	6	19%
Print Media	72	6%	2	6%
Electronic Media	30	3%	0	0%
Subtotal Paid Sources	425	37%	11	34%
Lead and Sales Subtotal[3]	1,150	100%	32	100%
Unknown Sources[4]	150	--	0	--
Total[5]	1,300	100%	32	100%

(1) Program-to-date leads
(2) Prior year sales
(3) Leads and sales with reported source
(4) Unknown lead sources excluded from calculations
(5) Percentages rounded

After you have tallied the stats, scrutinize the difference between lead source versus sales source; this data is essential in measuring the marketing program's performance and it is crucial to effective planning. Take a look again at Community A's analysis (Table 5) to see this concept in action. While community A uses a multi-faceted advertising program, the home run was hit by referral-based sources, constituting 63% of total leads and 66% of sales. Had Community A been consistently monitoring its lead and sales source profiles over the course of the program, it could have cut back its paid media without compromising sales.

The analysis findings also frame Community A's future marketing mix. Its lead generation tactics should be weighted more toward lower-cost, referral-based marketing and less toward higher-cost direct mail, print media, and electronic media.

Remember this marketing dictum: It is the source of sales that you want to perpetuate in your future marketing endeavors, and not just the source of leads.

Lead-to-Sale Close Rate

Now we come to the last aspect of our lead analysis—the close rate. Sometimes referred to as the "inquiry-to-close rate," this ratio is the percentage of qualified leads that are converted, or will be converted, to sales.

The close rate is used in two contexts: 1) as a gauge of the sales team's actual production (actual close rate=historical annual sales divided by qualified leads), and 2) as a performance target of the percentage of leads the team intends to close (projected close rate=sales objective divided by qualified leads). It is the projected close rate that is used in calculating the lead objective (lead objective=sales objective divided by projected close rate).

If these definitions and equations read like hieroglyphics, don't be concerned. Just follow the outlined steps.

First, determine your actual close rate by dividing your total sales per annum by your total qualified leads. The Lead-to-Sale Close Rate table in the *Marketing Plan Template* allows you to document five years of close rate data. However, you can limit your analysis to fewer years, as shown in the example provided for Community A (Table 6).

Depending on the year in review, Community A's close rate ranged from 2.4% to 2.8%, with an average of 2.5%. If you're thinking like a strategic marketer, you're probably asking: 1) Are these close rates good or bad? and 2) Which close rate should be used in the lead objective formula? The answer to both questions depends on the baseline (or target) used. You can compare your actual close rate to, and base your projected close rate on, the industry average close rate, which ranges from 2% to 5% of qualified leads. Or the baseline can be your team's actual performance—its "personal record," so to speak. In projecting ahead, you always want to set the close rate performance bar high. Let's use Community A's lead-to-sale close rates to find out why.

With its actual average close rate of 2.5%, you could say that Community A is doing an average (or acceptable) job of converting leads to sales when its performance is compared to the industry average range of 2% to 5%. However, you could also say the close rate is on the low side of the industry average. Had Community A's team been operating at the upper-end of the industry average of 5%, it would have closed out the prior year with 65 sales instead of 32 sales—more than enough activity to achieve full occupancy (1,300 leads multiplied by 5% close rate = 65 sales).

> Any time that you have a low or declining close rate, you need to find and correct the cause.

Also notice that Community A's close rate has been declining. This trend is significant—any time that you have a low or declining close rate, you need to find and correct the cause. A subpar close rate can be attributed to one or more of three factors: incompetent sales practices, insufficient sales staffing, or marketing barriers (as identified in the environmental scan).

COMMUNITY A
Table 6 Lead-to-Sale Close Rate

	Prior Year	Year 2	Year 3
Total Qualified Leads [1]	1,300	1,155	904
Total Sales	32	30	26
Close Rate	**2.4%**	**2.5%**	**2.8%**

(1) Program-to-date leads

The staff at Community A erroneously attributed the close rate decline to a reduction in the number of new incoming leads. The contemplated corrective action was to roll out a series of print ads to increase lead activity. However, the tactic was off target, because the problem had not been correctly diagnosed. The problem was incompetent sales practices. The tip-off was that Community A's team of two sales representatives generated nearly the same sales production every year, despite the fact that the number of qualified leads (and pressure to fill vacancies) was increasing every year.

Chapter 4 covers solutions for correcting subpar performance as well as other staff-related issues and challenges.

Closing In On the Lead Objective

If you're a community with an established track record, you determine your lead objective by dividing the sales objective by either the industry average or your actual (or projected close rate), whichever is higher. Here's the equation again.

$$\text{Lead Objective} = \frac{\text{Sales Objective}}{\text{Close Rate (\%)}}$$

If you're a new community whose close rate has yet to be established, or a community that's clueless about your close rate because you haven't kept track of your leads and sales in the manner described, you'll have to use the industry average range and divide the sales objective by anywhere from 2% to 5%.

As demonstrated in Table 7 (following page), the close rate that you choose dramatically impacts the lead objective.

Scenario I: Uses Community A's prior year close rate of 2.4%. The resulting objective is 1,708 leads (the sales objective of 41 divided by the close rate of .024 = 1,708).

Scenario II: Uses a 5% close rate—that translates to the program only needing 820 leads (41 divided by the close rate of .05 = 820).

The difference between having to generate 1,708 leads versus 820 leads is substantial and drives home how important the close rate (staff competence) is in shaping the intensity and direction of your marketing program.

COMMUNITY A
Table 7 Lead Objective

	Scenario I	Scenario II
Sales Objective	41	41
Close Rate	2.4%	5%
Lead Objective	1,708	820

Unless you have some monumental marketing barriers, you should always strive for a 5% or higher close rate. Here's why: A masterful marketing program establishes control over two interrelated variables—the number of leads generated and the number of leads closed. While lead generation tends to get all the attention in a marketing program, it's the number of leads closed (the close rate) that most influences the program's results. If the sales team is adequately manpowered and is competent in courting and closing its leads, then fewer leads are needed to fulfill the sales objective. If the team is understaffed, or if the team is not doing its job, then marketing has to work harder to procure more leads to compensate for the sales staff inadequacies.

Keep this maxim in mind as you plan your program: Before you spend time and money to generate new leads, you should close the leads you already have.

The Net Lead Objective

Whether the objective is 820 leads or 1,708 leads, don't be intimidated by the count; your sales are not going to be totally derived from new leads because you will secure anywhere from a little to a lot of sales from your current lead base. Factor these leads into the calculations—simply subtract your current qualified leads from the lead objective to obtain your net lead objective. Follow the example provided for Community A (Table 8) and use the Net Lead Objective table in the *Marketing Plan Template* to determine your program's target.

Community A has a lead objective of 1,708 with 1,300 leads in the database (Scenario I). When comparing current leads to projected leads (lead objective), Community A's marketing program will need to garner 408 new leads.

In Scenario II, the lead objective was 820. Community A already has 1,300 leads in its database, which means that it has more than a sufficient number of leads to support the sales objective.

Community A

Table 8 Net Lead Objective

	Scenario I	Scenario II
Sales Objective	41	41
Close Rate	2.4%	5%
Lead Objective	1,708	820
Current Leads	1,300	1,300
Net Lead Objective	**408**	--

Sum Up Your Marketing Coordinates

We've come a long way since the beginning of the chapter, so let's summarize some key points and touch on a few remaining items before moving on.

Your marketing plan originates with two elements: the sales objective and the lead objective. The sales objective is the number of sales/move-ins the program needs to secure to fill vacant units and offset attrition. It is a combination of vacant units plus attrition. The lead objective is how many leads you need to secure your sales objective. Use the *Template's* Lead and Sales Objectives Summary table to communicate the same for your program.

Optional Analysis Steps

You can go further and even forecast the number of new leads the program will produce from various lead sources. For example, based on its lead source analysis, Community A could project that 60% of its new leads will be generated via networking, 20% will come from direct mail, 10% will be generated through special events, and 10% will be derived from print media advertising. This breakdown isn't a shot in the dark. Like all other estimates, lead source forecasts have to be grounded in fact and your program's anecdotal data. To take your analysis this far, you need to know where your leads are originating in order to forecast how these profiles will be replicated or modified in the future. This intelligence requires clean historical data and a very evolved marketing information system.

You can also analyze and determine your "lead-to-tour" and "tour-to-close" rates to assess staff performance and to assign productivity goals.

Your "cost-per-lead" and "cost-per-sale," also known as marketing "cost-per-unit," are additional variables to assess, with the understanding that this level of analysis requires a long history of expense and return data (as measured in leads and sales). As with the close rate, the goal is to capture more leads and sales at a lesser cost.

Some communities believe there are "industry-average" costing ratios and attempt to seek out and use these ratios as a way to come up with a marketing budget for a new program, or to gauge the cost-effectiveness of a current program. The pursuit of shortcut ratios is a waste of time. Our industry is severely lagging in marketing information collection; standardized, published costing ratios do not exist.

Now if you're a tenured marketing professional who has traditionally monitored these ratios using your own program costs, go ahead and include them in your marketing plan. Otherwise, don't concern yourself with what other communities are spending, which doesn't apply to you anyway. *Inside Advice on Marketing Senior Housing* teaches you how to customize and cost out your own marketing, as opposed to assembling your program based on irrelevant ratios.

Turning the Numbers into Strategies

What you've accomplished in this chapter is to establish a quantifiable foundation of information on which to base your marketing program. That's the SMART path to occupancy—Specific, Measurable, Achievable, Realistic, and Timely actions. This foundation needs to be fortified with one final segment: the plan's strategy and tactics.

Pick up any textbook on marketing and management principles and you'll find a dozen different definitions on the meaning of strategy and tactics. We'll skip the textbook theory and hit the highlights of these principles with definitions that have been tailored to fit our situation.

The marketing strategy sets the tone for your entire program—it's a classification or ranking of your marketing program's intensity or aggressiveness. There are two strategies you can pursue:

> **A maintenance strategy** is called for when your community is at full occupancy (or at the occupancy goal) and you have a sufficient lead base and close rate to derive the targeted sales objective.
>
> **A growth strategy** is warranted for communities that are not operating at their assigned occupancy goal. To accomplish the goal, more sales need to be secured, either by increasing the close rate or by increasing the size of the lead base.

The marketing tactics are those techniques that you will use to achieve the plan's objectives. They are the program's core, planned and applied with purpose. These tactics essentially represent the critical components of marketing. You've worked through the first two components—the environmental scan and setting your plan's objectives and strategy. Both prepare you for the planning and physical implementation of the remaining marketing components you'll employ to fulfill the plan's objectives.

The remaining critical components are:

- Customer Service
- Marketing and Sales Manpower
- Marketing Information System
- Information Center and Resources
- Strategic Networking
- Special Events
- Creative Design and Copywriting
- Collateral Materials
- Paid Media
- Direct Mail
- Print Media
- Electronic Media
- Marketing Plan, Time Line, and Budget

Every marketing program must employ each one of these components to achieve marketing success. However, the intensity at which they are employed varies and is strategy specific. The key is to recognize which strategy is indicated and know how to modify these components to fit the situation. The upcoming chapters cover every aspect of marketing and how its critical components are manipulated to accommodate maintenance and growth strategies.

> The essence of marketing is the quality of the product, and customer service is how you communicate that quality.

Customer Service—The Core Of Every Marketing Program

It's no coincidence that customer service is one of the first components in the marketing lineup. The essence of marketing is the quality of the product, and customer service is how you communicate that quality. It costs little to implement, yet yields abundant benefits. Get it right and you have record-setting occupancy; get it wrong and it costs you business. So before we go bounding off on a discussion of how to perfect your sales presentation or produce a slick new brochure, let's cover the basics of customer service.

While customer service is a critical marketing component, it is the one component over which marketing has the least control and accountability. We know that it's primarily the actions and attitudes of the frontline staff that define a community's image and reputation. However, frontline staff don't report to marketing, they report to operations. Marketing's role is to work with management to implement or improve the customer service standards that are practiced by staff.

In reading through this chapter, you may find that you're familiar with many of the customer service concepts being presented. After all, customer service is really nothing more than good old-fashioned manners and business etiquette. However, the issue goes beyond your customer service expertise; it's about the staff's customer service understanding and expertise. For these very reasons, the chapter's principles have been deliberately fashioned so they can be shared with and easily understood by the entire team. At the chapter's conclusion, we discuss the ways the marketing department can contribute to community-wide customer service initiatives.

Customer Service Concepts

Think back on your environmental scan and the subject of your unique selling propositions, or USPs. If you identified and are touting "quality service" or "quality care" as a USP, you might want to think again about your use of these overused phrases. Just call a few communities and you'll find a whole lot of halo polishing going on—they all expound upon their kind staff and exceptional service as if they were extraordinary offerings. With so many providers mouthing the same words, consumers tune out the clichéd sales hyperbole and tune in on how they are treated. In fact, research has shown that customers tend to judge quality based more on the attitude and attributes of the person providing the service than on the actual quality of service being delivered—in other words, personal attitude trumps procedural efficiency. How many times have you encountered crackerjack service personnel whose dour faces would splinter if they attempted a smile? Or been served by someone who fumbled and bumbled his way through a transaction, but whose good nature made the experience acceptable and even pleasant?

> With so many providers mouthing the same words, customers tune out the sales hyperbole and tune in on how they are treated.

Staff need to be keenly aware that their actions and attitudes speak volumes about the quality of service that your community provides. The perceptions they create are more powerful than words alone. It's not enough to say that you provide quality service; it must be demonstrated in everything that everyone at your community says and does.

While service excellence is acknowledged by all communities to be central to their operating mission—it can be a challenge to achieve. The pursuit of service excellence and quality customer service can come off as so much fluff to staff who may be struggling to make ends meet, to get and from work, and to figure out who is going to care for their kids while they are busy taking care of others.

So how do you train staff on the necessities and nuances of quality service? An easy approach is to break service concepts and staff training down into the four elements that profoundly influence customer perceptions and satisfaction. We'll examine all four areas as a customer service training framework:

- Telephone Reception
- Physical Plant Appearance
- Staff Appearance
- Staff Attitudes and Actions

Top-Notch Telephone Reception

Telephone reception is the place where most customers form their first impression about your community. Create a bad first impression and what comes later, no matter how wonderful, must overcome a huge hurdle.

Managing the first impression is a tough task, especially in our business. Consumers have heightened service expectations when they contact service purveyors compared to product vendors. When it comes to senior housing, consumers expect to speak with someone who is professional, polite, and sensitive to their needs, someone who will listen to their problems and help them find solutions.

Answering the telephone promptly and professionally should be one of the easiest aspects of our business, yet this area is fraught with customer service land mines. Because of heightened expectations, seemingly simple telephone transactions can turn into appalling customer service transgressions. Innocent statements such as, "They've all gone home for the day" or "There's no one here right now, you'll need to call back," give the impression that your community is understaffed or uncaring. Making prospects listen to the entirety of The Beatles' "Hard Day's Night" as they wait on hold can quickly disenchant someone who is not all that enthralled with retirement living to begin with. Delays in answering the phone or encountering a rude receptionist or robotic voice mail are additional incidents that send consumer confidence into a nose dive.

So what are the solutions to these common problems? The answer is to use less technology and more high-touch personal service that is achieved through a blend of telephone protocols and training.

Let's start with the use of voice mail, a tool that is fine for business-to-business communications, but a disaster in working with senior consumers. Although voice mail is viewed as a cost savings measure, consider its cost in lost customers who refuse to use, or do not know how to navigate, this technology.

> Voice mail technology is fine for business-to-business communication; it's a disaster in working with senior consumers.

If your community uses voice mail as its primary greeter, then you need to go back to the basics. What did we do before voice mail was invented? We answered the phone—and we did it the good old-fashioned way, with a live receptionist, which is how our old-school customer prefers to do business.

Staff training on "what to say and how to say it" is also essential to creating an exceptional reception experience. Consider developing telephone "scripts" as a way to implement uniform standards, train new staff, and make it easy for long-term employees to brush up on their techniques. These scripts should address all primary greeter scenarios, from phone-ins to walk-ins.

Before you raise the bar on performance expectations or undertake any telephone training endeavor, be sure to revisit the role of your reception staff to make sure they have the time and resources to "deliver the script." A receptionist who is overloaded with a hodgepodge of duties and responsibilities will not have the time or the motivation to perform his or her fundamental function—to receive the public.

Also look at what hours receptionist coverage is available and when it's absent. A surprising number of communities still keep office hours that fail to accommodate the schedules of those customers who can't call or visit between the hours of 9:00 and 5:00. Your community needs to ensure that back-up phone coverage staff are provided scripts and training on the variety of after-hour telephone scenarios they are likely to encounter.

The Flawless Physical Plant

> It's tricky to sell a high-ticket item if the product doesn't look the part.

Similar to the first impression that's created by the initial telephone reception, the physical appearance of your community speaks volumes about the quality that's inside. It's tricky to sell a high-ticket item if the product doesn't look the part.

Some environmental imperfections are design or age related, such as long travel distances from the residents' apartments to amenity areas, or dark, poorly lit hallways. They can also be the result of budgetary chokeholds that show up in multiple ways—from the absence of decorative accessories and special touches to run-down furnishings that should have been retired long ago. Address these issues in the environmental scan.

However, most physical plant flaws are those we create and tolerate. Take a tour of your facility with the eye of a newcomer and you'll notice dozens of consumer turnoffs, from scarred doorjambs and soiled carpet, to hand-lettered signs taped to the walls. While sales representatives like to present their communities as the resident's home, imperfections can give the place a look that's a little too lived-in.

Marketing staff are often frustrated because it seems they are the only ones who see the community's environmental imperfections and they're always carping about what needs to be cleaned up, or scurrying about picking up to prepare for an appointment. Doesn't anyone else notice that the dining table condiment containers could use a thorough cleaning?

> It's not the newness of a community that counts—it's good housekeeping and maintenance.

These fixable imperfections occur for various reasons. It may be because staff know what to do, but get away with doing less. This can be especially true in older communities that have tired interiors. Work standards become relaxed. Staff feel it's impossible to make an old building sparkle and a few shortcuts here and there won't be noticed. Sometimes, staff have lost sight of what the community should look like. Coming to the same place day after day, they may not see the fingerprints on the front door, the scuff marks on the walls, or the messy bulletin board.

Or a community's imperfections could be because everyone has a different standard or interpretation of what constitutes a clean and orderly environment. What one individual sees as clutter, disarray, or dirt may go unnoticed by another. The varied and sometimes scary appearance of staff offices is a great example of the "diversity in cleanliness" concept.

Whatever the reasons for a community's poor appearance, you can be sure the customer sees it. It's not the newness of a community that counts in making the best impression—it's good housekeeping and maintenance.

So how does a community consistently present a top-notch setting? The first step is to find and correct simple-to-solve presentation problems: replace the tattered vinyl sign-in book at the front desk with a leatherette guest book, remove the hand-lettered signs taped to walls and doors, replace stained ceiling tiles, and touch up doorjambs and baseboards with a fresh coat of paint.

The next step is to define the standards of excellence for physical plant presentation—what the environment should look like and what to avoid, down to the details of making sure furniture is properly placed, newspapers are picked up, and lamp shades are straightened.

The need to have a plan that pays attention to the details is best summed up by the remark made by a resident who had just moved into a new community: "Just because this place is new doesn't mean it couldn't use a little soap and water now and then. I can't believe no one bothers to sweep the entrance every day."

Of course, the key to presentation success lies in training frontline staff to see and solve the problems. This is one aspect of customer service training where practical exercises add impact and fun to the learning experience. For example, have staff from every department take a tour of your community and offer a prize to the person who discovers and offers solutions to the most barriers. This walk around in-service combined with in-class training reinforces the concept that keeping the community clean and presentable is everyone's job, not just housekeeping and maintenance.

A Polished Staff Appearance

Of all the areas of customer service, it's the subject of dress code that tends to spark the most staff controversy. It is an emotionally charged topic and more complicated than in the good ol' days, when how one dressed for work or pleasure was well established and straightforward. Gone are the days of work clothes, play clothes, and Sunday "go-to-church" clothes, when women wore dresses and men wore the pants. Just think back to June Cleaver's attire in the television show *Leave It To Beaver*. She vacuumed the house in a dress, pearls, pumps, and a fresh apron.

Today's times are not so simple. Our closets are bursting with T-shirts, tank tops, crop tops, stretch pants, sweat pants, and dress pants. We have outfits for every occasion, every season, and every mood. Unfortunately, these wardrobe collections have found their way into the workplace. The result is a relaxed dress code standard and a less professional appearance.

Dress code controversy is compounded by managerial staff, who often represent the greatest hodgepodge of appearance. Those of the old school follow a rigid code of dress; others are more concerned with making a fashion statement. Body size often shapes a person's wardrobe choices, whether it is resistance to an "unflattering" uniform or a penchant for showing a bit of skin. If managers and department heads can't agree on what constitutes professional dress, how can they expect frontline service staff to know what constitutes appropriate attire for the workplace?

Another challenge is the staff-popular concept of "casual Friday" or "dress-down day," where it's okay to come to work in clothes you wear at home. While a relaxed dress code may be acceptable for the back-office staff parked in corporate America's high-rise cubicles, it's not all right for our industry. We serve a conservative and opinionated generation. When it comes to those who care for others, people do judge a book by its cover, and personal appearance sends a powerful message. As one prospective resident noted after being introduced to the community's administrator, "Oh! That was the administrator? When I saw her earlier, I thought she was the beauty salon operator!"

> Appropriate dress is defined by what customers expect to see, not what staff want to wear.

Dress standards don't need to be complicated. Appropriate attire is defined by what the customer expects, not what staff want to wear. Has your community bothered to ask the residents what dress they prefer?

Perhaps we should take a dress for success cue from other service industries, such as banking, hotel, and travel businesses. Rather than wearing street clothes, administrative personnel in these sectors present a "uniform appearance" with a themed wardrobe comprised of jackets, shirts, slacks, and skirts.

Marketing staff especially need to be the model of professional and appropriate dress. There's no way you can establish credibility with the customer if you don't look every inch the professional. Your attire should never speak louder than you do.

If our industry wants to maintain and enhance its service reputation, it has to raise the bar on dress expectations and define the standards for appropriate attire. Dress code policies need to be strengthened with an eye toward the details, and they need to be enforced. Be specific in prescribing your professional dress standards. Uniforms and street clothes should be clean, pressed, and appropriate—as in no stretched or gaping seams, not too tight, not too short, and fabric that is thick enough that you can't see a person's underwear. Name tags should be legible, free of artwork, smiley faces, and do-dads. Grooming standards need to get into the nitty-gritty—as in nails that are clean and trimmed, no offensive body odor (including too much cologne or perfume), and no visible body art or tattoos. Makeup should be simple, accessories minimal, and shoes and belts polished to a high shine.

> Dress code policies need to be strengthened with an eye toward the details, and they need to be enforced.

The bottom line is this: Personal opinions and preferences about professional attire need to be put aside the moment staff walk into work. If you have a dress code, enforce it. If you don't, establish one in conjunction with input from residents and staff.

Superior Staff Attitudes and Actions

Another customer service complication is the generation gap that exists between residents and the staff. On one end of the service spectrum we have the staff, a younger generation reared in today's high-tech times where quality service (or service of any kind) is a rare commodity. At the other end of the spectrum is the resident, raised in a time of Old-World courtesy when personal service was the primary commodity being sold.

Residents grew up in an era when gas station attendants washed their car windows, checked their oil, and inquired about their families. At small town grocery stores, clerks knew their names and personally filled their orders. Live telephone operators answered the phone and transferred their calls.

Today, self-serve gas stations have replaced the service station and supermarkets the size of football stadiums stand in place of the corner store. You're in big trouble if you don't own a touch-tone phone and aren't a master at voice mail maneuvering. Our society's pursuit of timesaving convenience—drive-through fast-food, dry cleaning, pharmacies, and dough-on-the go banking—has removed the personal service factor from our daily lives. It's little wonder so many businesses have customer service challenges; most younger staff have never experienced, nor are they exposed to, quality customer service in the world around them. So how do you train staff on the importance of creating a fine dining experience for residents when their reference point is a fast-food joint?

The key to enhancing customer service is to help staff experience and understand good old-fashioned manners and business etiquette. Etiquette fundamentally prescribes or restricts the ways individuals interact with one another and show respect for others by conforming to the norms of society. It is the rules for good behavior—and good behavior is doing business in terms the buyer can understand.

> The key to enhancing customer service is to help staff experience and understand good old-fashioned manners and business etiquette.

Written protocols should prescribe exactly how service personnel interact with customers, spelling out desirable attributes and attitudes, such as having a warm and approachable manner, being polite, and looking people in the eye. Involve residents by inviting them to provide an in-service about "what it was like in my day" so staff can get a sense of old-fashioned virtues and values. Try role-playing to introduce positive and negative body language and to train staff on words and phrases that elicit a positive customer response.

Marketing staff in particular should be the embodiment of Mr. and Ms. Good Manners. Tone down the high-powered, gushy, and touchy presentation and pace your style and presentation speed to the customer's personality. Contribute to the conversation without dominating the conversation. Be reserved on your initial approach and put a lid on your animation and enthusiasm until you get a feel for the personality of the person you're serving. Mrs. Smith is apt to be put off by an arm-pumping handshake; she comes from a more reserved world—she will extend her hand first as a signal that she is interested in pressing the flesh.

Remember, too, that formality is another way to show respect: Don't get too casual too quickly. Perfect your diction and articulation. Never call prospects or residents by their first names unless given permission to do so. Speak to them politely and kill the slang and contemporary vernacular such as, "you know," "yeah," "wow," "really," "uh-huh," "something like that," "okay," "cool," and "gosh."

Marketing's Contribution to Customer Service

Our industry isn't the only business attempting to return to the graces of good manners. You'll find an abundance of etiquette and good manner guides and training aids to reference on the subject. These materials offer humorous, real-world tips and techniques for training staff on every aspect of high-touch personal service delivery.

In addition to these tools, staff need training, training, and more training on all aspects of optimum customer service delivery. The pursuit of a customer-centered culture is an ongoing process, not an abbreviated staff-training program held at orientation or a one-time cheerleading session.

The best customer service training programs are designed by management and administered by department heads—they set the standards and the expectations, and ensure compliance. Management should survey staff ahead of time to determine program content and to create buy-in, remembering that those who do the work have the best ideas.

While the marketing department should contribute to implementing customer service initiatives, marketing should not be the program's sole champion or conduct all customer service training programs. Why? Because the marketing department does not have the authority to hold staff accountable to customer service standards. Also, when all or most of the customer service training programs are administered by marketing, good customer service is incorrectly viewed as an occupancy-development tactic, as opposed to an inherent aspect of day-to-day operations.

> Marketing should not be the sole champion of a community's customer service training program.

Marketing's role is to work with management to define exacting customer service protocols, especially as they relate to how incoming calls are answered and transferred to your department, physical plant and staff presentation standards, and staff protocol for interacting with guests that are being provided community tours. The marketing department should also be responsible for providing staff training and orientation on these same subjects. The customer service action steps in the *Marketing Plan Template* will help get you started.

Quality customer service is a critical component of operations and marketing that provides long-lasting benefits. The investment made in this area serves more than just your community and its residents. The real pay off is that staff develop pride in a job well done and a self-confidence that will serve them in all aspects of their lives.

> Occupancy success is dependent on individuals who want to sell, like to sell, and are highly motivated by the money they can make by doing their job well.

Marketing and Sales Manpower—How To Staff For Success

You'll enjoy this chapter because it's all about the marketing and sales team, from staffing models, ideal roles, and productivity goals to training and education, and best of all, various compensation programs. Forget about the old-school method of shaping your staffing based on a bare-bones budget and past practice. Rather, you'll learn how to fulfill your staffing needs based on your program needs.

To achieve the lead and sales objectives you identified in Chapter 2, you must resource your marketing program with ample, highly skilled manpower. The question, of course, is how much? Before you can define how many staff your program requires, you first need to determine what has to be accomplished. In fact, if this is your first go-round with crafting a formal marketing plan, you'll most likely need to configure your departmental staffing after you have worked through all the critical components and identified the key elements of your marketing plan.

The Five Essential Marketing Functions

However, there are five essential marketing and sales functions that are universal to any marketing program; these functions must be reflected in your ultimate staffing configuration. Don't get hung-up on the job titles. Give your attention instead to the described roles.

Marketing Director. Plans and puts into practice the entire marketing program, from performing the environmental scan to implementing the sales, networking, special events, and advertising campaigns.

Sales Representative. Responds to inquiries, performs lead follow up, provides tours and presentations, and secures the sales objective.

Marketing Assistant. Provides administrative support to the marketing and sales team.

Community Affairs Representative. Plans and carries out the program's outreach activities to support the lead generation and sales effort.

Move-In Coordinator. Provides post-close support services to new residents as they transition from their present homes to your community.

If your present departmental staffing mirrors the five essential positions, then you have the makings of an optimally configured team. If you're reading all of these positions and laughing out loud, it may be because you're the only person in the marketing and sales department—you're a staff of one. Chances are, the identified roles and functions are miles away from what management thinks your department needs or can afford. However, don't be discouraged. Now is the time to take charge of your situation using the information provided in this chapter.

Also, do not interpret these functions as black-and-white mandatory staffing minimums for all communities, or construe them as full-time positions. Rather, the goal is to match your staffing to the program's lead and sales objectives (and the assigned maintenance or growth marketing strategy) through a combination of positions whose duties are structured to allow the highest and best use of staff time.

For example, a growth marketing strategy, with its higher lead and/or sales objectives, would technically warrant a full-time marketing director whose sole role is to plan and execute the program. However, it may make more sense to secure the services of an industry marketing/advertising firm to provide the marketing director with supplemental support in planning and executing select marketing components, at least until the program is well underway. This support enables the marketing director to devote more time to higher-impact functions, such as managing the sales team and directly participating in sales.

A maintenance marketing strategy, with its more modest lead and sales objectives, can easily operate with a leadership position that has a dual marketing and sales role.

Rather than employ two higher-cost sales representatives who are responsible for a myriad of general administrative tasks that chew up valuable sales time, it makes more economic sense to hire one sales representative who is supported by a marketing assistant. A marketing assistant can take the clerical load off the sales representative by coordinating and processing the oceanic flow of paperwork associated with resident move-in. The assistant can also perform various administrative tasks, from maintaining collateral material inventories to event planning.

Networking can be accomplished by the marketing director, by a team of community personnel, or by a designated full-time person. Chapter 7, Strategic Networking, details how this marketing component is transacted and by whom.

Move-in coordination can be provided by a team of community personnel or by a designated full-time staff position. Depending upon the sales volume, the marketing assistant can also serve as the community's move-in coordinator.

The Team Approach to Marketing

It's not uncommon for board members, residents, volunteers, and management to participate and contribute to marketing in a variety of ways. In some organizations, these groups function in a formal marketing role, offering guidance and recommendations through committees, task forces, and ad hoc planning meetings. In other communities, they participate directly in frontline sales: Volunteers provide the sales team with clerical support; residents serve as the community's primary greeters (telephone and front-desk reception), provide tours, and show their apartments; while community departmental staff fulfill similar sales-related duties.

If your community uses a "team approach to marketing" (in the manner described), make sure it is pursued for all the right reasons and accomplished with the right structure. If non-marketing personnel or residents participate in the process, they should do so because they want to be involved, not because the marketing department is understaffed. Whoever is participating, all team members must be provided with the proper tools, training, and protocols to be effective representatives.

> A team approach to marketing should be employed as a supplement to, not a replacement for, requisite marketing personnel.

The bottom line: A team approach to marketing should be employed as a supplement to, not a replacement for, requisite marketing personnel.

Optimize Performance

Let's sink our teeth into some specifics on how to further maximize the effectiveness of your team, beginning with how you presently spend your time—and how to make better use of your time.

Too often, marketing and sales staff allow themselves to become distracted from their critical duties by a torrent of trivia and tasks. For example, many marketing directors spend too much time preparing ads, creating collateral materials, or planning the next special event. The busywork that is performed in the name of marketing comes at a high cost to the program. There is no way you can competently plan and execute an informed and integrated marketing program if you stay sequestered and separated from real-world sales. Stop fiddling around with writing brochure copy and get out from behind your desk to listen to how the receptionist is greeting the inquiring public. Instead of spending your time taking photos for your next newsletter, let a professional handle the job, and shift your attention to working up solutions to prospects' concerns. Start your day by preparing for the day. Instead of checking voice mail and responding to e-mail messages, huddle with the sales team to orchestrate priorities.

The Right Amount of Time

So how much time should you spend on marketing planning and implementation? It depends on the situation. If you're a corporate marketing director, the director of a new project that is preselling, or the director of a troubled community that is in "occupancy turnaround," then your role is exclusively that of providing marketing planning and management leadership.

If you're a community-level marketing director, you should devote no more than 30 percent of your time (on average) to marketing planning and execution and spend the balance of your time supervising the sales team and/or selling, and supervising and/or conducting the community's outreach efforts.

> You're supposed to be a marketing pro—meaning that it shouldn't take all of your time to plan and implement a program.

You're supposed to be a marketing pro—meaning that it shouldn't take all of your time to plan and manage the program prescribed in this book. As you read through *Inside Advice on Marketing Senior Housing*, you'll learn how to build a marketing flywheel that will make you more efficient and effective—to accomplish more in less time.

Sales representatives are easily sandbagged as well with a barrage of brushfires that can burn up a day—from troubleshooting the malfunctioning toilet in Mrs. Smith's apartment to finding Mr. Johnson's application and deposit check. Many of the critical tasks necessary to secure sales are ignored or incomplete when teams perform a hodgepodge of duties—attending meetings, ensuring unit readiness, and processing application and contract documents.

A sales representative should shoot for an 80–90 percent time allocation to pure sales. Pure sales tasks are defined as responding to inquiries, performing lead follow up, providing tours/presentations, and securing the sales objective. This performance standard can only be achieved if staff are insulated from the countless distractions that can erode their sales focus.

Productivity and Performance Goals

Let's assume the marketing and sales team has developed to the point where it is making the highest and best use of its time. The stage is set to assign each team member clearly defined performance goals for the number of phone calls they will make to their lead base, the number of tours they will provide, and the number of sales they will secure each month. This structure is important.

Those of you who work in the trenches know first hand that a move-in commitment is no easy decision for a senior adult to make; leading prospects through the process takes patience and guidance, countless telephone conversations, meeting after meeting with prospective residents and even with their family members. Hours are spent showing apartments, touring the community, and answering never-ending questions and concerns. Building this high-touch and time-intense relationship has been quantified into an industry statistic: It takes an average of five to eight consumer interactions to secure just one sales commitment.

Table 9 (following page) offers industry-standard performance goals based on the successful experience of hundreds of communities. If you're a seasoned marketing or sales professional, these telemarketing and sales guidelines will be familiar and likely reflect your own goals. If you're new to the industry or not accustomed to operating with productivity parameters, these goals will sound like sky-high, even unachievable standards. Or, you may be of the mind-set that you don't need to consistently interact with your lead base, or that structured prospect interaction constitutes high-pressure sales tactics. If that's the case, then you probably need to reconsider your chosen profession. Successful sales representatives don't need to be sold on the value of working with productivity goals and guidelines. They meet their marks without complaint and center their energy on creating opportunities to further build relationships. So don't dismiss these guidelines and assume that they don't apply to you; this production is commonplace. The *Marketing Plan Template* contains a table for you to document your telemarketing and sales

Table 9 Staff Performance Goals and Capacity

Monthly Task	Marketing Director	Sales Representative
Phone Calls	250	500
Sales	2-3	4-6

performance goals. You can also assign goals for the number of tours staff are to secure. In formulating your goals, keep in mind the provided telemarketing and sales goals are just industry averages, and there are no standardized guidelines for touring activity.

The key in assigning your goals is what works for you and your team, and what level of activity (calls and tours) produces sales. You'll need to consider the size of your lead base, your lead-management procedures (e.g., how often individuals should be contacted and by whom), and what other essential duties the team must perform, from networking to move-in coordination.

Above all, don't compromise quality for the sake of meeting assigned goals. The base premise is that every prospect interaction should be a thoughtful, meaningful, and personalized gesture.

Staffing Configurations and Capacity

The industry performance goals are also a tool you can use to back into the number of staff your department needs. Take a look at Table 9 again. We know that if a sales representative's duties are optimally configured (with 80–90 percent of the time devoted to sales), the staff has the capacity to secure four to six sales per month. A competent marketing director can contribute two to three sales per month. This assumes the marketing director is devoting around 30 percent of his time to program planning and administration, 50 percent to sales, and 20 percent to networking. Translated, that means a department of three full-time staff—a marketing director, a sales representative, and a marketing assistant—can produce up to nine sales a month, as well as fulfill the department's marketing administration, networking, and move-in coordination duties.

Use this "team of three" example to peg your own staffing model and productivity goals. If your program's sales objective is higher, the program will need additional sales personnel—one person for every additional four to six sales. A community that offers a continuum of care will also have greater and more specialized staffing needs and a sales director who is responsible for managing the team. If your sales objective is lower, the program could probably be serviced with just a marketing director (who also has sales duties) and a marketing assistant.

Whether you're tweaking or transforming your marketing and sales manpower, bear in mind that this is one aspect of your plan that won't happen overnight and without careful planning. You're moving into a territory where personalities, politics, and economics play a major role. You may have to make some staff changes with the understanding that the loyal person who has served your community so well for the past decade just isn't the right person to serve the needs of your future marketing program. Or, you may have to combat staff complacency and the antiquated attitude of "we-have-always-done-it-this-way," even when it is abundantly clear that "this way" isn't producing results.

The battle for resources may occur on the budget front against members of management who think it's possible to scrimp on marketing and sales manpower without forfeiting revenue in the end. If your community follows the Stone Age practice of employing just one person to perform all of the five marketing functions previously outlined, you'll need to convince management that developing a well-manpowered team is an investment, not an expense. This investment pales in comparison to the amount spent on misguided advertising or the income lost due to vacant units.

Your present staffing situation may not be your doing, but it is your responsibility to change your staffing if it's not sufficient to fulfill the needs of your marketing program. You have the blueprint—now's the time to step up to the plate and put together the right team with the right skills.

Training and Education

Staff training and education is the bedrock of any successful marketing program. It's especially indicated when you consider how most senior housing sales and marketing positions have evolved amid nearly absent educational resources. Take a look at most teams and you'll find staff with a variety of backgrounds. Some have crossed over from long-term care or social work. Others have a real estate or retail sales background. Countless positions are filled by individuals who were drawn to our industry because they once "took care of their grandmother" or "they like old people."

> Most staff are not adequately prepared or attitudinally attuned to work with seniors.

It's little wonder the number one prospect objection—the "I'm not ready yet" excuse—leaves most teams paralyzed. It's not surprising that as an industry we only close 2 to 5 percent of our lead base. Most staff are simply not adequately prepared or attitudinally attuned to working with the most powerful and discerning of all consumer groups—the senior market. Why? Because most teams have not benefited from formal marketing and sales training.

There are a couple of ways to enhance your knowledge and know-how. First, take the time to read the industry trade journals. These publications often feature articles on marketing and sales topics. However, don't limit your reading to just marketing-related articles. Take in everything you can about senior housing. The more you know about the industry, the more effective you will be as a marketer and a manager.

You can also attend state and national association meetings whose programs usually include marketing and sales sessions, some of which are intensive workshops and credentialing seminars. Peer networking during these meetings presents an opportunity to learn from the experience of others. You can also network locally. Make a get-acquainted visit or host a meeting of area marketing and sales staff to exchange information and to problem solve common issues.

How to Tackle Your Training Needs

While these resources are beneficial, they're too topical to fulfill all your training needs. Marketing and sales mastery can only be achieved through frequent and in-depth instruction. If you're a marketing veteran with a lot of off-the-shelf training materials, you've got the curriculum covered. If not, you'll need to secure the services of an industry marketing firm to meet your requirements. This avenue is the only way for novice staff to obtain the education they need.

> Marketing and sales mastery can only be achieved through frequent and in-depth instruction.

Take it from two industry marketing consultants—not all marketing firms are equally qualified. Be sure to examine the capabilities of any firm you consider, and research their experience in working with your type of community. For example, if you're a not-for-profit, entry fee based community, you don't want to engage a firm whose only experience is marketing for-profit rental retirement communities. Also check out the qualifications of the consulting staff that would provide the training. You don't want to hire an "experienced" firm only to find the assigned trainer has less hands-on sales experience than you do.

As the client, remember that you have control of the training content. You need to make sure the curriculum is not a rehash of boilerplate content—that it is consistent with your core values and community positioning, tailored to your needs, and designed to provide solutions to the problems that you're experiencing.

The hallmark of a reputable industry marketing firm is an operating philosophy that revolves around providing communities with the tools and training they need to do their jobs as opposed to doing the job for them through an extended and expensive consulting relationship.

A good working structure is to engage a firm to provide initial basic training followed by intermittent, in-depth training.

Design the educational modules to build the team's knowledge of the senior housing industry, the senior consumer, the sponsoring organization, the product, the marketing plan and program, protocols and procedures, and sales techniques.

Look at the training session outline (Figure 1). Notice the "macro-micro" approach. The topics begin with instilling an understanding of the industry and dovetail into specific selling techniques.

FIGURE 1 Sample Training Session Outline

The Representative as an Industry and Information Expert
- Industry origin, evolution, and present senior housing models
- The continuum of care
- Your competition and its weaknesses
- Your product and its unique selling points

The Target Market
- Target market profile and senior consumer psychology
- Key factors in selling to older adults
- Techniques to enhance communications with senior adults
- The senior consumer decision-making process

The Marketing Plan and Program
- Program overview, goals, objectives, components, and investment
- Departmental operating protocol and procedures

Selling Techniques and Procedures
- Sales mistakes to avoid
- The sales environment (phone-in, mail-in, and walk-in protocols)
- The first contact: opening statement, profile development, invitation to visit, how to present pricing information, and closing the conversation
- Prospect follow up: protocol for continued telephone contact, telemarketing tips and tricks, personalized mailings, and customized form letters
- The marketing information system: lead-management protocols and procedures
- The presentation and tour: preparing for the interview, initial reception, pacing information, feature and benefit selling, touring sequence, and wrap-up
- Answering objections
- Closing tips: when, where, and how to close

Money, Money, Money

Sales staff compensation has two components: base salary and commissions. The mix and amount is dependent on the local cost-of-living, the competitive characteristics of the marketplace, the marketing complexity of the community, and the operational philosophy of the community.

Base Salary

It's customary to pay a base salary. The amount depends upon your region, the local economy, and whether you have a commission program. When a commission program is employed, the base salary should be sufficient to cover general living expenses—with the understanding that an equal amount (or more) can be earned in commissions.

In major markets where competition is fierce, base salaries may well exceed standard cost-of-living expenses. In these cases, a qualified and experienced sales representative may have an annual base salary of $50,000–$60,000 or more.

There are no base salary benchmarks for communities that don't pay a commission. Marketing and sales salaries are determined within the context of other departmental salary structures or as deemed by management.

Commissions

When it comes to salary versus commission compensation, there are two schools of industry thought: those organizations that embrace and encourage commission programs, and those that do not. It is high time we realize that, as an industry, we are still embracing Neanderthal beliefs about the payment of commissions.

An underlying problem with the profession is that many individuals who are responsible for sales do not like to be thought of as a "sales representative"—the connotation being someone who is disreputable or who uses high-pressure tactics to make the sale. Unfortunately, this aversion to being associated with the sales profession affects staff performance and compensation levels. Staff are reluctant to "go for the close" and equally fearful of having a portion of their income tied to their sales performance.

> The industry is still embracing Neanderthal beliefs about the payment of commissions.

The management staff of organizations that don't employ a commission program compound the problem—maintaining that this form of compensation is inappropriate for their mission or culture.

Whatever the reason for a negative attitude about commissions, here are the facts: Occupancy success is directly dependent on individuals who want to sell, like to sell, and are highly motivated by the

Table 10 Sample Commission Scale

Sales Per Month	Commission Per Sale
One to Four	$500
Five to Six	$600
Seven or More	$700

money they can make by doing their job well. This premise is not in conflict with a mission of service, provided the staff work in a manner that is ethical and consistent with the organization's culture.

If your organization does not use some form of performance-based compensation, maybe now is the time to start. Would your staff welcome the opportunity to set and achieve their personal income goals? Are they willing to take financial responsibility for their performance? Are you willing to give the right staff the financial motivation that causes them to hit the ground running every day?

On average, typical commissions range from $500 to $1,000 per unit, but can go as high as $1,500 per unit, depending upon local market conditions, type of community (entry fee versus rental), and the sales objective (low to high). If your per-unit commission is below $500, you may want to rethink whether it provides sufficient staff motivation, especially if the base salary is low.

Marketing directors and sales managers receive commissions on sales they personally make, as well as receive an override on sales secured by the staff they supervise. Overrides can range from $100 to $250 per sale.

A sliding scale is a popular compensation model that motivates staff to increase their sales production. The key here is not just the number of sales, but the number and speed of sales. The more units sold per month, the higher the per-unit commission (Table 10).

One-half of the commission is generally paid at the time of resident contract, and the balance is paid at resident move-in. When operating within a presales environment, it's customary to pay the entire commission at the time of the reservation deposit; charge back any paid commissions for cancellations that occur.

Some communities tie commission or compensation to various occupancy levels. While staff bonuses are always a welcome benefit, the staff's base salary package should not be significantly dependent upon this form of compensation. Too many variables beyond staff control adversely influence occupancy and consequently staff income. If you go this route, it's also a good idea to tie operations staff to a similar bonus structure to keep the two departments in step on selling and delivering on promises made.

Now that you know how to configure, train, and compensate an optimum marketing department, let's turn the page and explore one of the team's most important tools—the marketing information system.

The MKIS brings together accurate and timely data to form a body of knowledge for marketing managers to plan, coordinate, and control their marketing programs.

Marketing Information System—The Science Of Decision Making

The critical marketing components that we have covered so far make it clear that you need to be able to lay your hands on a considerable amount of data to put a successful marketing program into place. You must collect, manage, and interpret information on your market area, target market, move-ins, attrition, lead and sales activity, and the productivity of your sales team.

While the scope of requisite data may seem daunting, the process of assimilating and analyzing data is easy if you use a marketing information system (MKIS). The MKIS brings together accurate and timely data to form a coherent body of knowledge for use by marketing managers to plan, coordinate, and control their marketing programs.

This chapter explores the architecture and applications of a marketing information system from the two perspectives of lead-management software and lead-management procedures.

We will also examine the various reporting aspects of an MKIS to illustrate the science of information-based marketing.

Lead-Management Software

Those of you who have been in the business a while remember the days when we used "lead cards" or "lead sheets" as the primary means of managing our lead base. These cards contained our notes about the prospect's situation and our corresponding sales actions, such as "made phone call," "mailed brochure," or "provided tour." We all had a different method for keeping track of our cards, filing them either by an assigned follow-up date—the good ol' tickler file system—or by the prospect's name or interest level. Whatever the method, we were always sure to keep our "hot prospect" lead cards close at hand.

We learned the hard way that our manual record-keeping methods were just too cumbersome when it came to managing a sizable lead base. Information was misplaced, follow-up calls were missed, and sales were lost. Since the data wasn't computerized and in an easily retrievable format, our marketing tactics were based on a best guess or what worked in the past; there was no way to relate the valuable information on those dog-eared cards and faded lead sheets to our marketing program.

Today, these elementary practices have been replaced by lead-management software designed to: 1) provide an effective and time-efficient tool to manage your leads, and 2) collect and report on your target market demographic and psychographic profiles, marketing program performance, and sales team productivity.

There are several lead-management software packages from which to choose, ranging from industry-specific versions to generic contact-management programs. You can do an Internet search to obtain a list of software sources, or visit the tradeshows at your state and national association meetings to locate the more reputable and experienced software firms. Be sure to stay with an industry-based software. Installing an MKIS is tough enough without having to spend time and money to cobble together a program that doesn't accommodate the unique marketing information needs of senior housing.

> The cost of lead-management software is less than what you're spending on Yellow Pages advertising and the benefits are far greater.

If you've already invested in lead-management software, then good for you. This chapter, along with the action steps in the *Marketing Plan Template*, tells you how to augment your software and data-management practices to make the most of this tool. If you don't currently use lead-management software, then you need to; its cost is less than you're probably spending on Yellow Pages advertising and the benefits are far greater. This chapter guides you in determining the software features that you need, and how to set up your MKIS once the software is installed.

Information Architecture

All lead-management software keys off records (or screens) that capture stock information, such as the prospect's name, address, and nominal profile data. Since these fields form the raw database of the entire MKIS, you need to expand the prospect record to comprehensively capture information in four areas:

- Demographics
- Psychographics
- Marketing
- Sales

Let's look at each of these categories, their corresponding data fields, and the information you can obtain from the individual and cross analysis of these variables.

As you read along, compare your current prospect record (whether electronic or hard copy) to the presented information to make sure you're capturing key data. If you find the suggested data fields are more than you presently track, it doesn't mean that you're in for more work. Think about it this way: You and your team talk with hundreds of prospects each year who tell you essentially everything you need to know to position your community and to plan your marketing program—from how they first learned of your community to what they like and dislike about it. If you're like most sales representatives, you record some, but not all, of this information on your prospect record. Most of the information, however, either stays in your head, or is buried in copious conversation notes—locations where the data can't be accessed or objectively analyzed.

The advantage of structured software is that it enables the team to comprehensively computerize all prospect information into a central source for easy retrieval and analysis. Instead of spending valuable time writing or typing everything out, the team enters information into the software's predefined data fields. The time saved allows the sales team to better manage its leads, and marketing has the information it needs to better manage the program.

Demographics

Beyond the standard contact information of the prospect's name and address, your demographic fields need to capture additional data, such as age, gender, marital status, housing situation (e.g., home, condominium, or apartment), net worth/income, and the prospect's location within your market area. Especially sensitive information, such as the prospect's age and income, isn't necessarily obtained during the very first contact; rather, the team needs to be on point during the relationship to capture this information when offered by the prospect—and as a result of artful profiling.

Sales reps use demographic data to further their relationships with their prospects. The marketer translates this data into actionable information to establish target market profiles, to capitalize upon draw patterns (market service area), and to direct the geographic reach of the program's advertising campaigns—information we covered in Chapters 1 and 2.

For instance, let's say you run a report on prospect zip codes and find that your leads primarily originate from six zip codes, whereas leads that translated into sales originate from two of the six zip codes. These two high-ranking zip codes should be the focus of your subsequent marketing efforts. Or you may discover that a respectable percentage of your prospects live in apartments. This profile presents a prime opportunity to go after this market segment with specialized networking, an event, or a direct mail campaign.

Psychographics

Do you remember the research methods that were presented in Chapter 1? The MKIS was one of them—the dynamic consumer-analysis tool that tells you how to best position your community and marketing program to fit dominant market profiles and preferences.

To make sure your system is designed to accomplish this market research, first round out the MKIS's data fields to capture the prospect's psychographic profile, including prior and present occupation as well as religious and other affiliations. This information is beneficial in designing marketing tactics and community programming geared toward these special-interest sectors.

> Make sure that your MKIS is designed to accomplish market research.

You'll also want to construct your data fields to track prospects' opinions about your product (unit types and amenities), services (type and intensity), and your financial program (price points and positioning). By aggregating prospects' interests, concerns, likes, and dislikes about your community, you can quantify what offerings have the highest market appeal and what offerings constitute marketing barriers, and identify the most practical solutions to those barriers.

For example, if your data fields are constructed to track prospects' interest in your various unit types, you can determine if your unit mix aligns with their preferences. If you capture reactions to your financial program, you can quantify the market's acceptance of, or resistance to, your pricing. You can also measure the depth of a selling point or a problem. For example, how many prospects have commented that your fees are too high? You obviously wouldn't modify your pricing structure based on what a few prospects say, but a sample size of several hundred individuals gets your attention. Since you're also gathering net worth and income data with the MKIS, you would look at the economic profile of price-resistant prospects to determine if their opinions are a result of an unwillingness, or an inability, to pay your fees.

Marketing

Marketing data is understandably a big part of the MKIS. Its multiple data fields have been outlined to provide direction on the information scope your system needs to cover.

Lead/Sales Source. As you learned in Chapter 2, lead and sales source data mapping is essential to formulating on-target promotional tactics. For effective and finely tuned planning, you'll need to specify every lead-generation tool that you use or plan to use in your marketing program. You especially want to avoid classing your lead-source data by generic categories. For example, instead of using the catchall phrase of "referral," you should identify every individual or entity by group classification (e.g., attorneys, churches, physicians), so you can target these primary sources as well as spot untapped opportunities. This detail extends to your paid media as well. Create fields to catalog all of your event, direct mail, print media, and electronic media campaigns. Be sure to measure advertising concepts, themes, headlines, promotional copy, and campaign timing, as well as print media section and page placement, ad size, and ad frequency.

The purpose of this data aggregation is to analyze and compare each medium's performance, and to identify high-performing geographic areas, market segments, and campaign elements. This is what target marketing is all about. Some of the better software programs even allow you to load the corresponding budget for each promotional category so you can analyze your cost-per-lead and cost-per-sale.

Contact Method and Date. Don't forget to add contact method and contact date to your data fields; these simple variables yield a lot of planning information. For example, what percentage of your prospects first contact your community by phone, mail, or "walk-in" (without a prior appointment)? In which months can you expect the highest traffic? In which months do you realize the highest advertising returns? How many individuals are contacting your community after-hours or on the weekend? This information is used to shape office hours of operation, staffing requirements and schedules, lead-management protocols, and the timing of advertising campaigns.

Lead Status. Explaining this aspect of the MKIS gets a bit tricky because we all use so many different and subjective terms to describe our leads and their interest levels. Let's first define "lead status" and then look at specific status code examples.

The term "lead status" is a classification of the qualifications and disposition of your leads. A "qualified" lead is an individual who is of the appropriate age and health status to reside at your community and who has sufficient financial resources to afford living there. This definition should be familiar—it was introduced in Chapter 2, when we discussed using your qualified lead count to calculate your lead objective. Qualified leads are also referred to as "active" leads. Non-qualified leads are referred to as "inactive" leads.

"Disposition" is an additional gradation that communicates the prospect's tendency or inclination to consider and select your community. It is a ranking of interest level, and it is most often articulated in a time frame that indicates when a prospect is likely to move to your community. Unfortunately, this aspect of lead status is plagued by ambiguity—and ambiguity doesn't mix well with an information system. To hear the common classifications used by sales teams to describe a prospect's interest level is like listening to a weather report—with lots of chatter about "hot," "warm," or "cold" prospects. These descriptors generally correspond to a decision-making time frame: "30 days," "60 days," "90 days," and "future."

While there is nothing wrong with these rankings, they are somewhat incomplete. What we need to know is: "when and why." When does the prospect plan to move (assuming they are qualified), and if it is not in the immediate future (one year or less), why not? Disposition codes clarify the when and why. Take a look at the following examples and the benefits of definitive status codes become clear. These codes begin with prospect qualifications (e.g., active) and a disposition is appended to these qualifications.

- Active: New Lead—Not Yet Classified
- Active: Immediate Interest (1 month or less)
- Active: Highly Interested (1 to 3 months)
- Active: Somewhat Interested (4 to 6 months)
- Active: Interested (7 to 12 months)
- Active: Indifferent (1 year or more) "Not Ready Yet"
- Active: Indifferent (1 year or more) "Want to Remain at Home"
- Active: Indifferent (1 year or more) "Waiting to Sell Home"
- Active: Indifferent (1 year or more) "Shopping Around"

If you're accustomed to coding your leads as "hot," "warm," "cold," or by time frame, you'll notice the correlation between your classifications and the provided descriptors. For example, "Active: Immediate Interest" is equal to "hot," "Active: Highly Interested" is equal to "warm," and so on, until you reach the lowest classification, "Active: Indifferent," the equivalent to the classification of "future."

It is the "future" group that poses the greatest marketing and sales challenges. It's not uncommon for most prospects to tell you they are not interested (at least right now). For that reason, the "Indifferent" status code includes an attitudinal disposition so you can understand why a prospect isn't interested or is waiting so long to make a move, for example, "Waiting to Sell Home" or "Shopping Around."

All of these instances warrant continued follow up until a sale is secured or until the lead is deemed inactive. Whatever you do, never base your follow up date on the prospect's status code. Just because Mrs. Murphy's status is coded as "Active: Indifferent, Not Ready Yet" doesn't mean that you only contact her every six months or so. Prospects like Mrs. Murphy need the most cultivation so they can understand the prudence of joining your community now, not a year from now.

> A skilled and well-trained team will assess and reassign the lead status with each contact, moving the prospect from preliminary interest to a close.

Also bear in mind that lead status is not a fixed classification. A skilled and well-trained team will assess and reassign the lead status with each contact, moving the prospect from preliminary interest to a close.

Now take a look at example inactive status descriptors.

- Inactive: Can't Afford
- Inactive: Frail Health
- Inactive: Died
- Inactive: Moved Elsewhere
- Inactive: Do Not Contact (in cases where a consumer is explicit about not being contacted, in any way)
- Inactive: Mail List Only (in cases where a consumer does not want to be contacted by phone but is agreeable to receiving your literature)
- Inactive: Does Not Meet Residency Criteria (age, medical, or financial)

These descriptors are merely an outline of the definitive status codes that you need to create and customize for your own community. This assignment is worth your time and attention because good status codes have multiple applications and benefits. They provide a real-time comparison of the number of active leads in the pipeline in relation to the lead objective. You can compare lead status to lead source to monitor and continuously improve the types of leads that your direct mail, print media, and electronic media campaigns are generating. You can even devise advertising tactics around dominant dispositions. For example, if a large percentage of the active lead base is classed as "Active: Indifferent, Not Ready Yet," the answer is to raise prospect interest through stepped-up sales interactions, events, and direct mail marketing, subjects that will be covered in upcoming chapters. You could even implement a series of seminars that focus on overcoming this common prospect objection.

Sales

This MKIS category is where you catalog the multiple transactions that you conduct with a prospect from contact to close. These include phone calls, interviews, tours, information mailings, application and contract documents processing, deposits, reservations, and sales. In this category you also record what actions need to be taken with prospects and when.

Teams that work with an automated lead-management system start their day by running a report that tells them whom they need to contact. This function ensures timely and consistent prospect follow up. The staff's "planned-to-actual" progress in meeting their assigned productivity goals can also be assessed.

Sales data has marketing planning applications as well. Compare the qualified lead count to sales to determine the team's individual and collective close rates. If the close rate is below goal, the MKIS data will help you determine if the cause is due to a barrier or to substandard team productivity. It can even be the basis for requesting additional manpower by objectively demonstrating to management the staff time required to manage and maximize a sizable lead base.

Lead-Management Procedures

Lead-management procedures are the second aspect of a comprehensive MKIS. They prescribe how the team works with the lead-management software and its leads. We'll start by providing you with some tips on general data management, and then cover software protocols and prospect procedures in detail.

Be sure to stay abreast of software updates and technologies to better manage your information. Continuously review and update your networking, event, and advertising data fields to correspond to your present and planned programming. Periodically review demographic and psychographic descriptors to ensure that they reflect accurate and current market profiles.

One by-product of a good lead-management software (and system) is that it creates a comprehensive mail list to use in multiple ways and in multiple aspects of your marketing program. While your mail list grows each time a prospect name is added, be sure to think beyond your prospects to include all market segments that represent sources for referral-based leads. These include residents, residents' family members, individuals on the wait-list (if you have one), and the multiple market area resources that can refer, or have referred, someone to your community. Later chapters will show you a myriad of creative ways to court and cultivate these sources.

Software Protocols

After you have established or enhanced your software data fields, step back and think through the protocols for information management. How will prospect data be entered, when, and by whom? How will you ensure that correct and complete data is being captured by the team? How will this data be translated into information to help you manage the marketing program, the sales process, and the sales team? What reports will be generated and how will they be used? Pay particular attention to defining the coding criteria for the data fields that affect your marketing program, such as prospects' interests and concerns, lead sources, and lead status.

The team then needs to be trained on the software's information scope, its use, and the correct application of the data codes. There's a saying in data analysis: "Garbage in—garbage out," and garbage is what you'll end up with if data fields are not clearly understood and correctly used by the team.

Here's an example of how lead status classifications can be misused and misconstrued. Most teams try mightily to ascertain the attributes and interest level of each lead on the very first contact, usually over the telephone. Individuals whom the team believes are not interested or not qualified are either not pursued or not pursued for long.

> Sales teams are overly aggressive in devaluing their leads and prematurely screen out prospects as "not qualified".

This inappropriate telephone triage makes the sales staff overly aggressive in devaluing their new leads; they prematurely screen out prospects as "not qualified" and incorrectly classify them as "inactive." If this practice goes unchecked, the community's "inactive" lead count will eventually equal or exceed the "active" lead count.

A lot of communities receive thousands of inquiries (over several years), but due to poor sales practices have only several hundred active leads in their system. The sales staff grows panicky and complains they do not have enough leads to fulfill the sales objective. The unthinking reaction is to advertise more, with the intent of generating more leads.

If you're a marketing director who supervises a sales team, you need to be aware that every sales team wants more leads and better leads. But what makes you think that the next 10 individuals who inquire are going to be any different from the last 10 individuals who inquired? They're not. More advertising is never the answer to this kind of situation. The solution is to improve sales practices and establish protocols that can help police and prevent bad lead-management habits.

Prospect Procedures

Optimum lead-management software, combined with solid sales skills, is the genesis of good lead-management protocols. You're complementing your competencies with operating procedures that reinforce sound sales principles and help avoid common mistakes.

Before you go to work to draft your department's lead-management protocols, revisit your staffing configuration to ensure that your department is adequately manpowered. Remember that protocols are intended to maximize a team's resources and productivity, not prop up a poorly resourced team. For example, if the department's hours are limited to weekday coverage, this might be the time to consider whether you need sales coverage on the weekends or for extended times during the workweek. Many teams report that they do not receive weekend and after-hours traffic, but how would they know? They're not there!

> Protocols are intended to maximize a team's resources and productivity, not prop up a poorly resourced team.

Also, if other departmental staff are being called upon to provide backup sales support (information presentations and tours) beyond an intermittent basis, this too is a reason to consider adding more manpower.

If you work alone, and you're good at what you do, then you don't need a textbook-sized policy and procedure manual. A written summary of standard practices will suffice to orient team members, such as receptionist staff and contributing departmental staff, about their roles in the sales process. For example, establish protocols to ensure the receptionist does not send prospects information by mail instead of having them speak to you. Although the receptionist may think she's simply complying with a prospect's information request, what she's really doing is hindering your chances of getting the prospect in for a personal presentation.

If your community offers multiple care levels, the receptionist should not try to identify the prospect's area of interest or need, and the caller should not have the burden of identifying a level of care. Remember to keep your primary-greeter protocol simple; the role of the receptionist is to receive the public and get the inquiring public successfully transferred to the sales team, not do your prospect profiling and selling for you. These same rules apply to any community representative, whether it's a resident, staff member, or volunteer who interacts with a prospect on behalf of the sales team.

You're in for a bigger writing assignment if your department employs multiple staff. All the tasks and transactions of prospect interactions—specifically when, and how often the team will interact with prospects over the course of the relationship, need to be defined. These operating protocols are the uniform rules the entire team follows.

Look at Figure 2, an excerpt from Community A's Marketing Policy Manual. It gives you an idea of how good lead-management procedures go hand-in-hand with expert sales practices.

These detailed instructions put all team members on the same presentation page. For example, a well-trained sales representative will never blab to a prospect about all the services the community offers, yak about every unit type, or recite prices for every apartment. Nor will he ask a lot of needling questions to ascertain if the caller has sufficient health and wealth to qualify for independent living. Instead, he warmly engages the prospect in a conversation, builds rapport through thoughtful profiling and listening skills, and culminates the call by securing an appointment for a personal visit. Your lead-management protocols need to reflect this sales sequence.

A good sales representative also knows that it's her responsibility to take the prospect from preliminary interest to a higher level of interest, and finally to a close, by following protocol that results in sustained prospect follow up. The old saying, "Sales is a numbers game," is true. Besides skill, sales success is all about the numbers—how often a sales representative thoughtfully interacts

---

FIGURE 2 Sample Lead-Management Protocols

- Engage the prospect in a conversation, build rapport, and culminate the call by soliciting/securing an appointment for a personal visit.
- Do not disclose detailed information on unit types, services, or fees, unless you have a thorough understanding of the prospect's profile and can tailor information to his or her specific needs and interests.
- Enter every contact into the system, regardless of the prospect's qualifications. Minimum information should include full contact data, lead source, lead status, and an assigned follow-up date (for leads classified as "active"). For contacts deemed "inactive," be sure to select a data field that reflects the reason for the classification, (e.g., "Inactive: Does Not Meet Residency Criteria").
- If an appointment cannot be secured, send an information packet within 24 hours. It should include: a customized letter or note, brochure, and one or two floor plans that reflect the prospect's preference.
- Avoid mailing pricing information, more than two floor plans, application, or contract documents.
- Assign and enter a follow-up date in the system; the first follow-up should occur within five to seven days of the initial inquiry (applicable to "active" leads).
- Work to raise the prospect's interest level and secure an appointment with every re-contact.
- Update the prospect's record to include actions taken and changes in the prospect profile; reassess and reassign the status code and follow-up date with every re-contact.
- Re-contact the prospect at a frequency indicated by the situation, but no less than once every quarter. Permissible reasons to terminate contact or code as inactive include: death, moved elsewhere, prospect is adamant about "do not call."

with his or her prospects to help lead them through the decision-making process. That's why experienced sales professionals don't cringe at the notion of "dialing and smiling" every day. They know that with every phone call they make, and every presentation they provide, they are one step closer to achieving their sales objective.

> Good sales representatives know that with every phone call they make, they are one step closer to securing a close.

Some sales staff flat-out refuse to work with lead-management protocols and performance goals. We've all heard the representative who boasts that he slam-dunks sales all month long without following procedures and the tedium of ongoing prospect cultivation. This isn't something to brag about; it's a sure sign of an amateur and an underachiever. Here's the point: If a representative can produce sales using incorrect protocols imagine what he could achieve if he practiced good sales techniques.

Persistent prospect follow up is another area that sales staff sometimes resist. They believe they are being "pushy" if they call a prospect more than a couple of times. They back off the moment a prospect expresses indifference or disinterest, code the prospect as "inactive," and switch over to the easier role of processing new leads—until it gets to be uncomfortable again and the cycle repeats itself.

If protocols, productivity goals, and sustained prospect cultivation make your sales staff squeamish, maybe they shouldn't be in sales. To shortcut these fundamental aspects of lead management means they are shortchanging your community.

We've covered the importance of telephone sales protocols, but this venue is just one of many areas where you need to establish prescribed expectations. Protocols should be in place for:

- Walk-In and Mail-In Inquiries: initial contact and follow-up tasks
- Presentation Preparation: public areas, staff offices, and model apartments
- The Interview: primary-greeter and reception functions and where to conduct prospect warm-up/profiling
- The Presentation and Tour: the standard tour route, which apartments to show, what areas of the community to exclude from the tour, and staff protocols for interacting with guests
- Post-Tour: prospect follow up—frequency and corresponding tasks
- The Close: application and contract preparation and approvals
- Post-Close: transactions that take place up through resident move-in; identifies the point of resident transition from marketing to operations staff

- Marketing Information System: lead-management software applications, data field definitions, data entry, and reporting procedures
- General Administrative: community and departmental policies
- Back-Up Staff Coverage: secondary team personnel and prescribed inquiry-management procedures

It's a big undertaking to establish or augment a lead-management system. If you're a marketing pro and have the time to devote to the project, you can upgrade your MKIS on your own. However, if you have not benefited from professional sales training and are not rock solid in your sales skills—no offense, but you don't have the knowledge to put a MKIS into place. In this case, consider the support of an industry marketing firm. The use of an outside expert is also indicated for the busy manager who knows what needs to be done, but simply doesn't have the time to do it. An economical and effective approach is to contract for a turnkey work scope to obtain requisite sales, software, and lead-management training in one sweep. For a modest investment, you and your team can be expediently tooled with the very best sales practices and protocols.

The Wait-List

If your community maintains a wait-list (also known as a "futures list" or "reservation list"), you're going to need similar processes to manage this group along with your prospect base. However, before defining optimum protocols, let's take a hard look at some common wait-list practices.

The concept of a "wait-list" is somewhat controversial in our industry; those who don't have one want one, and those who have one are fiercely protective of it. Still others find them to be a bogus process that is fraught with marketing liabilities.

What's interesting is that a wait-list is really a double-edged marketing sword. It can either help increase demand for your services by implying the success of your community, or it can turn off prospective residents who lack the time and inclination to wait.

The advantage of a wait-list is that it provides a ready supply of prospective residents from which to derive move-ins. The result is a reduction in the turnaround time on vacant units (and lost income). Another important, but less tangible advantage, is the successful image a wait-list instills in the mind of the market. A sense of urgency is created if your community is indeed "a preferred destination."

However, there are some real disadvantages to maintaining a wait-list. Communicating that you have a wait-list can cause a decline in referral activity. Potential prospects don't bother to inquire because they've heard that you're full with a wait-list. This perception is particularly damaging if you're sitting with vacant units and a dwindling, nonproductive list.

For communities that have true pent-up demand, as in no available apartments, a wait-list can create negative perceptions and even ill will. When faced with a long wait, individuals can become frustrated and angry if they are ready to move immediately or if they hear that someone else lower on the list was offered an apartment before they were.

A wait-list can also hamper your sales and marketing efforts. Staff are hesitant to engage in even the most basic activities, such as calling individuals on their wait-list, for fear of creating yet more interest that can't be served. Marketing paralysis sets in and suspended activity can lead to a softening waitlist and ultimately occupancy decline.

For all these reasons you need to be deliberate in how you manage and market your wait-list (if you have one), and careful to consider whether this strategy is right for your community (if you want one).

If you have vacant units, you don't need, nor should you offer, a wait-list. If you have a wait-list, then you need to assess its integrity by asking yourself two simple questions: 1) Are you waiting for the prospect to make a decision to move in, or is the prospect waiting and wanting to move in as soon as her apartment of preference becomes available? and, 2) Do you have vacant apartments?

> If you're waiting for prospects to move in, then you have a worry-list, not a wait-list.

If you're waiting for the prospect to move in, then you have a worry-list, not a wait-list. The truth is, those individuals on your list who are waiting to move in because they "aren't ready yet" are, in reality, prospects. By allowing a prospect to go on a wait-list, especially if you have available inventory, you have, in effect, validated and supported the prospect's inclination to procrastinate. So why give these prospects permission and a formal method (being added to your wait-list) to indefinitely defer their decision? This concept applies to any kind of list (e.g., "futures" or "reservation" lists) that gives prospects a way to wait for an apartment when you have inventory that needs to be sold. Instead of adding these prospects to some bogus list, you should work to secure a close as you would with any other prospect.

What about those fortunate communities that have legitimate pent-up market demand (for all units or a particular unit type), evidenced by full occupancy and a wait-list of individuals who are literally waiting to move in? How do you continue to market your community and maintain a wait-list without creating unmanageable demand or consumer frustration over the inability to access your community? In this scenario, you have several dozen to several hundred individuals on the list, a low apartment turnover rate, and it's going to be several years before individuals move up the list and move into your community. If your list has become unmanageable or is a marketing liability, consider the following options to cull or reduce your list.

Don't add future shoppers to the list. When you have a long wait-list, you attract individuals who are not ready to move anytime soon—they simply want to get their name on your list because they've heard that it takes several years just to get into your community. Don't encourage the practice by adding their names to your already too-long wait-list. They are no different from any other "I'm-not-ready-yet" prospects who tell you they are "interested for the future," and you manage them no differently.

Increase the wait-list deposit or increase the nonrefundable portion of your deposit. Most prospects don't think twice about plunking down a modest wait-list deposit of a few hundred dollars, especially if it's refundable if they change their mind. However, a deposit or cancellation penalty that is in the range of several thousand dollars flushes out those with serious intentions from those who are casually considering your community. If Mrs. Smith isn't willing to pay a respectable deposit as a good-faith gesture of her interest and intention of moving into your community when an accommodation is offered, then she most likely is not a legitimate wait-list candidate. Large deposits are an excellent way to differentiate the shopper who is interested in moving two to three years down the road from the individual who wants or needs your services now.

Rather than base the deposit on some arbitrary amount that is the same for all apartments, tie the deposit to a percentage of the apartment's entry fee, or an amount equal to the security deposit. Interest should be paid on all deposits.

Temporarily close the list. It doesn't make much sense, nor does it represent good business, to keep accepting applications and deposits from individuals if they have an immediate need that you can't soon fill. By continuing to accept applications from individuals that you can't immediately serve, you're fueling an already tenuous situation. If you temporarily close your list, you're not turning away business—you're portraying yourself as a responsible and ethical operator. What you're saying to the market is, "I cannot assure you access anytime in the near future, therefore I am not going to take your money." If you go this course, you must carefully plan its implementation and how you will continue to court these individuals until such time the wait-list is reopened.

Sustain interest and commitment. Involvement with prospective residents must go beyond the token biannual phone call to determine their continued interest or to offer a vacant apartment. You should know as much (or more) about these individuals as you do your prospects and seek ways to involve them in the lifestyle being offered. For example, make sure wait-list individuals are maintained as a "target market" in your direct mail database so they can be selectively integrated into your networking, special events, and paid media programs. You can also create a club or membership program that further galvanizes this group and that offers special perks, such as the use of your dining room to entertain guests.

Now you know all the twists and turns of database management, from software applications and lead-management protocols to the science of information-based marketing. Let's go from theory to practice and take a tour of where all of this work goes down: the information center.

> A less-than-ideal sales environment sends out all the wrong cues. Prospects need a plush setting to help buffer the shock they'll experience when they first hear your prices.

6

Information Center and Resources—The Ideal Sales Environment

This chapter is loaded with techniques and tools to create a superb sales environment. It covers everything from where you work to what you show prospects who visit your community. We'll also explore the concept of market-ready units and the essential tools and resources you need to establish an effective sales platform.

Let's start with the practical and easy-to-implement aspects of this critical marketing component and discuss something as simple as what you call your work area. If you use the term "sales" or "marketing" to refer to your office, consider what message that sends to prospects. In their minds, they're entering the sales zone—a pressure cooker where they will be "sold to" by a bunch of hard-driving sales reps. We know that isn't true, so why use phrases that cause prospects to conjure up these images? The phrase "admissions office" is equally alienating. It invokes all sorts of images, from a mental institution to a college campus, neither being a place where a senior consumer wants to reside.

Why not refer to your working area as the "Welcome Center" or "Information Center?" These descriptors are non-threatening to the prospect and do a better job of expressing exactly what transpires in these settings.

Make sure your selected direction is comprehensively applied to all signage and collateral material, and is used by all staff.

Now look at the physical setting of your workplace. Most of us operate out of offices that pull double duty—it's where we work with prospects and at the same time handle all of our behind-the-scenes paperwork and administrative functions. That's a problem from the prospect's point of view. Unfortunately most staff work in very small offices that are furnished with all the wrong stuff—oversized desks, scant seating, and lots of clutter. This less-than-ideal environment sends out all the wrong sales cues.

For example, if you sit behind a desk when working with a prospect, you've created an immediate barrier. How can you build rapport when a prospect feels as if she's addressing a superior instead of an empathetic community representative? Unsightly stacks of papers, boxes, or equipment piled around suggest to the prospect there is not enough space to store these items—and that resident storage space might be limited as well (both of which are often the case). Too many personal nick-nacks draw attention to the staff, instead of putting the focus on the prospect and the community. Uncomfortable seating, inadequate lighting, and poor ventilation or temperature control are additional sensory assaults that can make a prospect want to make a break for the door to return to the comforts of their spacious and well-appointed home.

Most senior adults would probably be willing to "sit on hard chairs to save some hard cash." However, the cliché doesn't apply to our industry. Prospects need a plush setting to help buffer the shock they'll experience when they hear your high prices. Incorrect sales practices can also compound a prospect's discomfort and disinterest. The biggest sales offense is to work with your prospects in any place other than a completely private setting. If you presently share your office with other staff or with noisy office equipment that needs to be accessed by other staff, or if you use a public place (e.g., the lobby or other amenity area) as your sales office, you're spinning your sales wheels. There's no way prospects are going to be at ease in these environments. Don't interpret their tolerance of the situation as interest in you or your community. They are just being polite while planning an early escape.

The Single Suite Solution

So how do you create an environment that has you looking at your watch wondering when the prospect will leave, instead of the other way around? The setting you create depends on the number of staff in your department and the office space available in your community. Several options are provided that range from an all-in-one office setting to a full marketing and sales information center.

If you're a solo sales representative working in a community where office space is severely limited, then you'll need to transform your private office into the information center. Here are the specifications.

The ideal information center is the most spacious and well-appointed office in the entire community. "Well-appointed" means on par with the administrator's or executive director's office furnishings, or the same caliber of appointments that are in the community's common areas, whichever is nicer. It should be a windowed office that is close to the lobby. Preferably it should have a pleasant view or tasteful window treatments to disguise an unpleasant view. Use residential-style furnishings instead of commercial or office furnishings—an open-front, low-profile desk and/or a small conference table with comfortable seating is preferred.

> The information center should be the most spacious and well-appointed office in the entire community.

Keep the visual emphasis on the community. The only artwork allowed are sales tools that portray your community offerings and can include professionally illustrated, framed, and well-lighted floor plans, level plans, renderings, and reservation/sales status boards. These visual aids provide a convenient way to orient prospects to the community's physical layout before going on the tour.

If you're operating on a shoestring budget and new furnishings are not an option, then make the most of what you have. Eliminate clutter and keep piles of paperwork out of sight when you know you have a prospect heading to your office. Arrange what seating you have so you can sit next to the prospect instead of behind your desk. Kill the fluorescent lighting and use a table lamp to add warmth and to communicate a sense of home. Above all, keep your office clean and presentable.

The Multi-Suite Setting

There are several ways to establish the ideal sales environment for communities that employ multiple staff. First, identify an area to serve as the dedicated information center. This area is also referred to as a "warm-up" or a "closing" room, which essentially describes what goes on here.

It should be appointed with your best furnishings: a conference table and either a love seat and/or comfortable chairs and side tables. Natural, ambient and task lighting are a must. Some degree of accessorizing is fine—for example, an attractive beverage service set to offer your guest light refreshments. Have selected collateral materials on display (no pricing or floor plan information though), and a supply of contract documents stored nearby for fast retrieval. You'll need the same visual aids as described for the single-suite setting.

A model apartment can be equipped to serve as a backup location when the information center is in use by another sales representative or to take advantage of any buying signals the prospect expresses while on the tour.

By installing a centralized information center, the team's physical workspace can then be located in individual or shared offices. This arrangement lets staff work comfortably without the pressure of keeping their offices in a constant state of readiness. A separate working office also provides a place for the sales rep to put her head down and work the phones; when not working the phones, she's with a prospect in the information center or model apartment, making a presentation, or providing a community tour.

You can also temporarily or permanently convert one or more vacant units into a self-contained suite to house the information center, model, staff offices, and resource area. This approach is a practical alternate use for apartments that are difficult to sell due to their design, location, or views. A lot of providers balk at the idea of using income-producing apartments for what is seen as a non-income-producing role. However, the loss of revenue is offset by the income from the additional sales the team produces.

Whatever design you select, the team needs to be resourced with all the tools and equipment to perform the administrative and lead-management aspects of the job. This means adequate filing and storage space, a sufficient number of phone lines, telephone headsets, high-speed printer and copier, a fax machine, and computers to access the lead-management software, e-mail, and the Internet.

An item that isn't on the resource list is equipment to play marketing videos or DVDs. If you think about it, marketing videos or DVDs are a cold way to warm up prospects or recap your presentation. Electronic presentations are also a transparent sales tactic; prospects are aware that they are being baby-sat while you're busy with another customer or off taking a short break. Electronic collateral materials are fine for long-distance sales with individuals who can't immediately visit your community. However, this high-tech tool should not be used as a surrogate for a high-touch presentation.

> Marketing videos or DVDs are a cold way to warm up prospects or recap your presentation.

The Ideal Model Apartment

An extension of the information center is the model apartment. Citing economic reasons, some communities show residents' apartments instead of setting up a functioning sales model. This is especially common in communities that are full and have a wait-list—they don't want to lose income by converting an apartment into a model. Other communities use a resident's apartment (instead of a model) because they take pride in showing off the lifestyle that residents enjoy, and think residents are equally excited to let others see how and where they live.

So is the use of a resident apartment the best practice for showing a model lifestyle? Probably not, and here's why. Before you go knocking on Mrs. Smith's door with a prospect in tow, stop for a moment and think about the situation from Mrs. Smith's perspective. Sure, she said you could show her apartment anytime, but does it have to be right now? How many times has she had to open her door to you and a stranger while in the middle of meal preparation, her favorite TV show, an afternoon nap, or just as she was stepping out to go shopping? Instead of living the "retirement life" where she can do what she wants when she wants, that morning call from the sales office sends her scrambling to gussie up for you and your approaching guest.

> It's not a good idea to use a resident's apartment as an example of a model lifestyle.

Then there's the issue of Mrs. Smith's privacy. She may not want strangers opening closet doors, peering into cabinets, and tiptoeing around the bedroom and bathroom. A well-mannered prospect will be uneasy about doing so. These areas are private spaces, filled with personal items—from the old robe and shower cap hanging on the back of the bathroom door to the countertop cluttered with denture cups and arthritis creams. You get the picture, and so does the prospect as she backs out of Mrs. Smith's bathroom.

Consider, too, the prospect's impressions. The residents' furnishings may not reflect the prospect's taste or are arranged so that it's difficult to see the apartment's size and layout. Even if the apartment is decorated in keeping with the prospect's taste, the ambience created by family photos and a lifetime collection of memorabilia can derail the reason you're there in the first place. A simple comment by the prospect about an interesting piece of furniture can snowball into Mrs. Smith's detailed account of how this cherished possession was passed down from her great-grandfather and how she's not sure where it will go when she passes on, because, you know, her son, who lives in Denver, isn't too interested in such things, and here's a picture of the boy standing with her dear departed husband, and (sigh) she doesn't mind that her son visits only once a year; after all, there are lots of ways to occupy her time now that she lives at your community.

Model Standards

Remember that your prospects didn't come to your community to get a lesson in antiques or to hear stories that remind them of the painful aspects of growing old alone. They came because they needed a solution to their own unique problems.

Instead of showing an occupied residence, create a separate model apartment that demonstrates to prospective residents how they can make their own place to call home. Here are some tips to get the most out of this valuable sales tool.

- Instead of filling the space with hodgepodge furnishings, think about how you would use the space if you were to live there and furnish it accordingly. Install realistic appointments of the proper size and scale to fit the living space—a prospect is quick to spot downsized furnishings or impractical pieces that have been placed to mask a small living space.
- If you haven't already done so, solicit the services of an interior design firm or furniture company to decorate your model in exchange for subtle advertising.
- Create an inviting ambience with classical music, potpourri, fresh flowers, or the aroma of a freshly brewed pot of coffee. Also make sure that you always have beverages and snacks on hand.
- Be sure to prepare the model before any presentation—turn on lights, straighten pillows, replace hand towels, put the toilet seat down, and open or close drapes (depending on the view).
- Use artwork and accessories to add warmth and to draw the prospective resident's eye around the room or away from problem areas. For a few hundred dollars you can supply your model apartment with all the "personal comforts of home," such as eyeglasses on a bedside table, house slippers beside the bed, a good book, a comfortable throw on a side chair, and attractive bathroom and kitchen linens.
- Keep a sharp eye out for any barriers that may deter a sale. If the view is problematic, use decorative window treatments to draw the eye into the room.
- Encourage your guest to have a seat, relax, and absorb the setting and all the information you have covered. Now is a good time to conduct some "trial closes."

Show and Tell

At some point, it is routine to show prospective residents a vacant apartment, either as an example of the unit type being considered or as the apartment they've selected. Success in showing apartments is part product and part sales competence. If you're not careful in what you show and what you say, you run the risk of sabotaging the sale. Let's discuss product readiness first, and specifically, market-ready units, a concept first introduced in Chapter 2.

Market–Ready Apartments

A lot of communities will defer vacant apartment refurbishment until such time that a new move-in is secured, or the maintenance and housekeeping staff can work unit repair and cleaning into their schedules. This practice presents a problem for marketing. The sales team cannot be expected to sell what they can't show, and the team should never show a vacant apartment that is not in pristine condition. Allowing a prospect to see a unit that has not been refurbished since being vacated by its last occupant is a sure way to lose a sale. Nor will the team produce sales when their time is spent making sure they have presentable product to show.

> Never show an apartment that is not in pristine condition.

So what is a market-ready unit? It's an apartment that has been freshly painted, the carpet and window treatments have been cleaned (or replaced), the plumbing, mechanicals, and appliances are in working order, and the apartment is immaculate, from its windows, floor, and appliances to its lighting fixtures.

This level of unit-readiness is what is usually in place before a resident moves in. The market-ready concept is based on the premise that vacant units are rehabbed to move-in condition before they are shown to a prospect.

The team should always have market-ready units to show and sell (if there are vacancies), and these apartments should be in place one month or less after being vacated. The suggested time frame is not just about fulfilling marketing's needs—it's about increasing revenue by decreasing vacant unit turnaround time.

Marketing, management, maintenance, and housekeeping need to work as a team to create an environment and product that helps, not hinders, the sales efforts. The team needs to define unit-readiness standards and the procedures for vacant unit preparedness. The team also needs to identify what staff are responsible for implementing these standards without a lot of unnecessary follow through by marketing to make sure the job gets done.

The Right Way to Sell Apartments

Even though your vacant units are now up to par, that doesn't mean you are going to show a prospect your entire inventory thinking that you're doing a fine job of explaining your offerings. In the end, a prospect will select just one apartment; overloading a prospect with an array of styles and locations simply causes confusion and mental fatigue. Your job is to lead prospects to a decision to join your community, not confound them into indecision. Only show prospects what they can afford and what they want. If you don't know their preferences, then you haven't done your homework.

Of course, most prospects want the largest apartment you have to offer and that they can afford. However, no matter what size apartment they are shown, most prospects are likely to crinkle their nose and note that it is just "too small." This is a typical and predictable comment, and you need to expect and be adept at overcoming this objection. The wrong sales response is to thumb through every floor plan and run around looking at every unit type. The right way to respond to space and size objections is to understand their present situation, what rooms they use, and what problems they are trying to solve (such as high utility bills and home upkeep), and artfully articulate how your homes are a thoughtful solution to their needs.

The sales environment for senior housing has to look and feel like an invitation to a highly desirable lifestyle, and the team needs to feel good about where they work and what they have to work with. A well-appointed and comfortable information center, an appealing model, and spotless market-ready apartments set the stage for a performance that gets rave reviews from the customer and sales team alike.

A well-designed and consistently intense networking program will outperform advertising in its ability to generate leads and sales.

Strategic Networking— The Kind Of Publicity That Money Can't Buy

Strategic networking is a new twist on an old marketing standby—grass roots promotions. You might know it by other names: community outreach, community affairs, or referral-based marketing. "Strategic" means that your efforts are integrated with every aspect of your marketing plan. "Networking" implies a deliberate and highly structured method of building market awareness, one individual and one organization at a time. This chapter looks at the many ways this fundamental marketing component is used to increase the quality and quantity of your leads.

Before we get into specific networking techniques, let's step back and look at how networking strategically fits into your overall marketing plan. So far we have covered six critical components. They have been deliberately sequenced to prepare you for the promotional phase of your marketing program. You have learned whom to target (environmental scan), how many leads and sales you need (objectives), and how these leads and sales will be serviced (customer service, manpower, MKIS, and the information center).

The next component, strategic networking, is an important mile marker, for it represents the point where the marketing program actually shifts into its promotional phase. You're now ready to address how leads will be generated through networking and the remaining marketing components—events, collateral materials, direct mail, print media, and electronic media.

Networking in the Scheme of Things

A marketing program is designed to generate leads using a blend of promotional components, from networking to direct mail, print media, and even electronic media. Your lead and sales source profiles and the assigned marketing strategy determine the intensity with which these promotional components are employed.

Networking, however, is the only component whose use is consistently vigorous during the life of the marketing program. Why? Because collective experience has taught us that over time, a concentrated networking initiative will outperform paid advertising in its ability to generate sales. This phenomenon moves strategic networking to the front of the promotional pack.

> The more leads that you derive from referral-based marketing, the fewer leads you need to generate through paid media.

The value of networking is made clear if you think of it this way: The more leads that you derive from referral-based marketing, the fewer leads you need to generate through paid media. You can see this concept at work when you look at a community's age and the promotional mix it employs.

For example, suppose that your established community enjoys a high referral volume as a by-product of its strong reputation and years of service. The referral volume is so strong, in fact, that it's sufficient to support the lead objective. In this case, you would use strategic networking to further leverage established relationships and sustain referral momentum. You would use paid media minimally, as a way to maintain market awareness and to make up any potential lead objective shortfalls.

Now consider a situation where your community is newly opened or is in pre-marketing. You're at ground zero on lead activity of any kind, especially referral-based leads. Although you would implement networking to establish relationships and further the community's reputation, it will take time to carry out and realize any appreciable results.

In this circumstance, you would need to use paid media to expediently shore up the lead base and to achieve the sales objective. As your community's reputation grows, so does the referral volume. This volume, in combination with your ongoing networking, begins to supplant the need for paid advertising.

Chapter 7 Strategic Networking–The Kind of Publicity That Money Can't Buy

Although veteran marketers all agree on the value of networking, we also know that it's usually the first aspect of the promotional program to fall apart or be put on the back burner. It's hard to justify spending time to build relationships to generate leads if your community is already blessed with abundant inquiry activity. A word of warning: Allow yourself to become comfortable with this good fortune and you're dead, they just haven't buried you yet. Full occupancy means you must forever look over your shoulder and look ahead to protect and maintain your market share.

Another reason networking efforts stall is that they're time consuming and logistically rigorous. You can't sit back and wait for the phone to ring. Strategic networking demands that you reach out to the community to communicate, one-on-one, with those in your various target markets. The activities are numerous: telemarketing and letter campaigns to solicit meetings and presentations, site visits to drop off everything from gifts baskets and brochures to mugs and magnets, presentations that must be written and made. One glance at this to-do list and it's easy to understand why networking tasks are deferred to another day.

Networking also takes nerve. The marketing director who talks easily to the single prospect may turn timid when faced with "cold calling" new groups or when standing in front of 20 individuals peering over their bifocals and raising their hands to ask prickly pricing questions.

It's no wonder that so many marketing directors default to the quick mechanics of placing an ad as their primary means for keeping their community's name out there. It's easier. However, stand firm—resist the temptation to let your advertising program do all of your lead-generation work for you. Remember that while all communities need to advertise, it's an adjunct to, not a replacement for, solid grass roots networking.

> Don't confuse strategic networking with resident festivities, public relations, open houses, or making doughnut runs to doctors' offices.

All that said, networking doesn't have to be a tedious and time-consuming assignment. With the proper systems and administration, it can be a simple and seamless process. Let's look at how this is accomplished.

First, don't confuse strategic networking with resident festivities, public relations, open houses, or making doughnut runs to doctors' offices. Its scope is much greater and more structured. The scope is in the sheer number of groups you will contact. The structure is the plan that you use to guide your efforts.

A good networking plan identifies your focus markets, stipulates when and how you will interact with the identified groups, and generally covers what will transpire during these transactions. The Strategic Networking Planner in the *Marketing Plan Template* contains these and other key elements to help you initiate a new networking program or provide ideas for enhancing a program that is already in place.

Primary Focus Markets

Since networking is such a time-intensive activity, it's imperative that you rank, according to referral value and volume, the groups with whom you want to network. Essentially, you need to concentrate your outreach efforts on those individuals and groups who refer the most leads—your focus markets. While there are exceptions, your primary focus markets are your residents, your waitlist and prospect base, followed by residents' family members and friends, and then on to staff, board members, and volunteers. By starting with sources inside your community, you not only save time, you are also working those groups with the most potential to refer leads. Plan and work your program from the inside out. This is efficient and effective networking at its best.

Here are some ideas for how and when to interact with these primary groups.

Residents

The most effective programs for encouraging resident referrals are those that get the residents involved. Testimonials are the conventional method—they are both believable and credible—but be creative in how you use this resource. Featured testimonials don't have to be limited to a clichéd one- or-two-line quote in your newsletters and print ads. Why not have a resident write and sign a letter that is mailed to like-minded prospects? How about inviting a resident to join you at a prospect luncheon to speak to the group about the experience of living at your community?

Another traditional tactic is to offer residents an incentive (money or gift) to make referrals. However, residents don't want to be bribed into supporting their community, they simply want their community to be successful and the common courtesy of being acknowledged for the assistance they provide. Incentive programs tend to be more effective if the reward has altruistic value. In return for a successful referral, you might offer your residents a choice between a financial reward or a donation to their favorite charity. Or, how about hosting a "friend-raiser" (a variation on a fund-raiser) where residents are awarded a token that has an assigned dollar value for each referral they make? These tokens can be used to purchase an item selected by the resident for the community, such as a large-screen television.

> Resident referral programs tend to be more effective if the reward has an altruistic value.

Some communities offer prospective residents a move-in incentive—for example, one-month's free rent or a discount on the monthly service fee. The effectiveness of these programs as a motivating factor in causing someone to select and move to a community is debatable. A senior consumer is probably not going to make a life-changing decision over a few hundred or even a thousand dollars. What is most likely happening is that the timing of the customer's transition coincides with the timing of your monetary incentive. So sure, he'll take the money, wouldn't you?

But that isn't to say prospects don't need a lot of emotional support with decision making—and a little physical assistance doesn't hurt either. Many communities offer programs to help prospective residents overcome the monumental hassles of moving into their communities. Marketed under a variety of names (and different vendors), these programs provide an array of helpful services that include assistance with downsizing furnishings and years of accumulation, realtor representation, packing, moving, and the setup of the residents' furnishings in their new homes. This helping hand is either provided free of charge (as an incentive) or at a substantially discounted fee. The cost to the provider is nominal in relation to the exponential returns: faster inquiry-to-close time frames, more sales, and great reviews by satisfied customers who are more than willing to tell their peers about their positive experience.

Keep in mind that your residents can contribute more than just referrals. They can open doors for you. Find out to what clubs they belong, what churches they attend, where they do their banking, and where they went to college. If asked, residents can often get you on their organization's meeting agenda so you can make a presentation. They're also a good source for obtaining organizational and club membership lists to add to your MKIS database for select inclusion in your direct mail marketing campaigns.

> Keep in mind that your residents can contribute more than just referrals.

Whatever your incentive program, remember that for most people, a gracious "thank you" is sufficient. Practice good manners and be sure to send a handwritten note, flowers, a good book, or some other personalized gift to express to residents your appreciation for their contributions.

Wait-List and Prospects

If you've implemented, or are in the process of implementing, the MKIS procedures described in Chapter 5, then you should be at the top of your game in building relationships and interest with individuals on your wait-list and in your lead base. They are prime referral sources. We all know how quick Mrs. Carter is to tell you about her friend and neighbor, Mrs. Jones, who "needs to be at your community more than I do because Mrs. Jones is older and is looking a bit frail these days." Of course, what Mrs. Carter doesn't know is that Mrs. Jones is saying the exact thing about her! It doesn't matter that these individuals are referring each other because you're going to court both, along with your entire wait-list and lead base in a variety of ways.

These groups require more than a sales "follow-up call." You have to constantly look for and create opportunities to interact with these individuals. Invite prospective residents to your events, or better yet, ask them to speak at an educational program. Include them in all your newsletter mailings, and recruit them as volunteers.

Residents' Families and Friends

> It's better to spend $25 on a thoughtful gift than to spend $250 to advertise in a fringe publication.

Next are the residents' families and friends. These individuals are particularly important sources for those communities that also offer assisted living, long-term care, or community-based services, such as home care. Nurture these relationships through frequent and consistent communications.

Add the names and addresses of family members and friends to your MKIS database for inclusion in newsletter and event invitation mailings. Always acknowledge the referral support of family and friends with a thank-you note or small gift. It's better to spend $25 on a thoughtful gift than to spend $250 to advertise in some fringe civic-group publication.

On the day a new resident moves in, have the apartment refrigerator stocked with snacks, and offer a complimentary lunch or dinner to those assisting with the move. Some communities provide new residents with fine stationery or pre-printed postcards to notify family and friends of their change of address. Add a few more amenities to these suggestions and you have a complete hospitality program designed to help residents feel welcome, ease the transition to their new homes, and increase resident satisfaction.

Staff, Board Members, and Volunteers

Staff, board members, volunteers, and auxiliary groups should always be encouraged and provided with the proper resources to tell your story and send referrals your way. Orientation and ongoing education for these key constituents will give them the information they need to effectively and professionally represent your organization. Furnish a small stock of select collateral materials (newsletters and overview brochures) for distribution. Scripts are also helpful to tactfully suggest what message you want to convey and what information to avoid (e.g., pricing).

Similar to your resident referral tactics, see if board members can suggest you as a speaker at a club, community group, or institution to which they belong. Don't forget to solicit membership directories for use in direct mail marketing; (wouldn't it be great if you could get your hands on your local university's alumni directory?). This tactic may cause privacy concerns, so be sure to check the organization's membership list disclosure policy. Some organizations will make their membership list available for use if the requesting entity is sponsored by a member, provided they understand how it is being used and they're able to see the relevance and appropriateness of information that is being sent to their members. In some cases, they may even allow you to add your literature to a mailing of their own.

Getting your systems in place to court and cultivate the preceding groups is a sizable undertaking that may require an entire year to fully implement, especially if you don't have a full-time position dedicated to networking. That's all right—take your time, think the program through, and do it right. Networking with these sources alone will go a long way in buoying your referral activity.

Secondary Focus Markets

Once you're consistently courting your in-house sources, it's time to reach out into the community, where there are literally hundreds of organizations, entities, and individuals that have the power and potential to send customers your way. These include churches, civic and fraternal organizations, bankers and lawyers, employers, medical practitioners and healthcare institutions, realtors, media representatives, and even morticians.

Prioritize these groups by their referral value: those close to home, those who represent your target market (by age, income, and affinity), and those suggested by your residents or board members.

If your community offers a continuum of care, you'll also need to calibrate your outreach efforts to your various offerings. For example, medical practitioners, while somewhat beneficial to independent living, are essential and top-ranking referral sources for assisted living and long-term care referrals.

> Don't bother networking with Gary's Gun Club or the Tuesday Night Bowler's Association—their members won't be moving to your community anytime soon.

The lowest-value groups, and those you can skip, are organizations whose membership profile is completely off the mark from the target market you want to reach. For example, don't bother with Gary's Gun Club or the Tuesday Night Bowler's Association—their members won't be moving to your community anytime soon.

The referenced groups are a partial listing just to get you started; the Strategic Networking Planner in the *Marketing Plan Template* provides a comprehensive list of potential referral sources for you to consider and customize to your community.

Smart Networking Steps

Community outreach is most often associated with the arduous task of making "cold call" contacts and speaking presentations. However, there are a myriad of ways—and easier ways—to establish and leverage community-based relationships.

The first step is to put together a list of all possible referral sources. This can be accomplished with the assistance of volunteers or a marketing intern from a local college who compiles contact data using information furnished by residents, the Yellow Pages, and a Chamber of Commerce directory.

Your initial outreach should be in the form of a phone call. When you contact each identified organization, be careful how you introduce yourself and how you explain the reason for your call. Any communication that smacks of a sales pitch will meet with a closed door. Keep in mind that networking is about more than generating leads. If you do it right, you're presenting your community as something other than a place where "old people" live. You are portraying your organization as an involved community partner and an informed resource on the subject of senior living alternatives. It's hard to reject someone who is calling simply to get acquainted and exchange information.

> Keep in mind that networking is about more than generating leads. If you do it right, you're presenting your community as something other than a place where "old people" live.

During the conversation, you want to learn as much as you can about what the organization does, whom it serves, and how. This will help you identify how you can potentially assist its members. At the same time, you want to provide an overview of your community and suggest ways to work together.

For example, in addition to making a presentation, you can exchange articles of interest for inclusion in newsletters or other publications. You can also offer your community as a meeting place, as cosponsor of an event, or as host for a special event. Collaborative marketing tactics are further discussed in the next chapter.

What you learn and accomplish during this first contact essentially determines what you do next and when. At the very least, you should add the names and addresses of these groups (if appropriate) to your MKIS database so you can continue to educate and build interest through newsletters and event invitation mailings.

However, do not commingle these contacts with your wait-list and prospect database. They should instead be stored as a separate file within your MKIS database. To allow easy access and assimilation in targeted mailings, be sure to establish and sort your contacts by descriptive categories, for example, churches and trust officers. If you don't have lead-management software, then you should maintain your list using software that has mail list management capabilities.

The Speaker's Bureau

You can facilitate your outreach endeavors by establishing a speaker's bureau of specially selected and trained staff. This team approach to networking requires good procedural structure and sufficient staff resources to ensure that the speaker's bureau gets beyond the "good idea" stage. You'll need to prepare, or help staff prepare, speeches of approximately 20 minutes in length on topics of interest to your primary and secondary focus markets. You should also prepackage and provide presenters with all associated program materials (handouts, collaterals, and leave behind tokens) as well as provide a way for presenters to capture attendee names, which will then be added to your database. Just because your community offers the services of a speaker's bureau doesn't mean the phone will ring with presentation requests. This service will only be used if the public knows about the resource. It must be promoted, and opportunities for speaking engagements must be solicited.

Public Relations

You may have noticed that the subject of "public relations" hasn't been referenced thus far in our critical components of marketing, and you won't find it discussed much later on. That's because it's not a formal marketing component. Rather it's a by-product of a comprehensive marketing program.

A lot of people within our profession use the terms "public relations" and "marketing" synonymously. Or they believe that public relations is a separate function from marketing, the typical reference being "marketing and public relations." This view is outdated. Public relations is, simply stated, the art and science of building relationships between an organization and its key audiences. Notice the similarity between this definition and that of strategic networking. If you engage in networking, as defined herein, you're covering your public relations base. If you implement a marketing program that contains the promotional components of networking, events, direct mail, print media, and electronic media, you're generating "publicity" about your community.

> Public relations is not a formal marketing component—it's a by-product of a comprehensive marketing program.

Instead of drafting a public relations plan, what you really need to do is network with your local media to obtain publicity that doesn't have a price tag attached to it. Here's how.

- Develop a list of the editors and reporters of local newspapers and keep it current. Do the same for radio and television, concentrating on those who regularly cover local interest stories.

- Maintain these sources in your database and treat them as any other community group. First, call to introduce your community, then make a get-acquainted networking visit. Take along your information brochure as your "media kit."
- Present yourself as an expert on the senior adult market who can serve as a ready source of information for age- or industry-related stories.
- Send press releases, your newsletter, and other direct mailings (as described in the upcoming chapters).
- Instead of waiting for media outlets to contact you or take notice of your mailings, take the reins and furnish ideas for a series of stories or a feature story. Our society is just now realizing the vast implications of the "age wave," and the media, as well as other businesses, are becoming more interested in this newly discovered market. Take advantage of this trend to show off your senior-consumer experience and wisdom, and to spotlight your community.

Roles, Goals, and Performance Standards

Chapter 4, Marketing and Sales Manpower, identified networking as an essential staff function. To be clear, networking is not a discretionary activity that is accomplished if and when the staff has time. It's a mandatory marketing component that must be accomplished either by the marketing director, a designated full-time position, or by a team of community staff.

The scope and reach of your networking endeavors, along with your community positioning, ultimately define the staffing model to employ. For example, multi-facility organizations and providers that offer multiple care levels (from home care to long-term care) warrant, and can justify, full-time outreach personnel to work the multiple markets these organizations serve. In the case of a single service (independent living or senior housing) community that has a department manpowered by a marketing director, one or more sales representatives, and a marketing assistant, networking falls under the purview of the marketing director. If you're it when it comes to marketing and sales, then you won't have the time to perform outreach. Your community will have to use a team approach.

After the program has been established and staffed, it must be sustained through well-defined performance goals. These goals can be communicated as a time allocation (devoting a certain number of hours per month) or by task (contacting so many community groups per month), or by making a designated number of presentations per month. The base goal is to interact with as many groups as possible, as often as possible.

Before you put pen to paper to write your networking plan, be sure you work through the rest of the chapters that cover the critical components of special events, direct mail, print media, and electronic media. They must all work together as a unified force, rather than each existing in isolation. The concept is known as integrated marketing communications (IMC). Read on to learn how it's used to create program momentum and synergy.

Exceptional event planning creates something extraordinary out of the ordinary and generates excitement about your community like no other promotional component can.

8

Special Events— Programs That Pique Market Interest

A special event is a tool that enables you to attract the market's attention, maintain prospect relationships, and encourage prospects to purchase. By creating something extraordinary out of the ordinary, well-planned programs—from cooking classes to book signings to fashion shows and fun runs—generate excitement about your community like no other promotional component can. This chapter explains all the steps for turning out memorable events and the kind of events that gain patronage.

The planning and execution of this critical marketing component requires creative thinking balanced with practicality. Often referred to as "event marketing," the program goal is to increase traffic, leads, and eventually sales, using a bit of cachet and a splash of showmanship.

The practical aspect of event planning is in selecting the type of program that you will use to inform audiences about your community. You have two choices: educational events and social events. The creative aspect is in the promotional theme you use to pique the market's interest.

Let's look at how to put a good event together, from concept to completion.

Educational Events: A Multi-Faceted Forum

Educational opportunities, such as seminars and workshops, appeal to multiple audiences and serve a variety of purposes. Seminars for your wait-list and lead base are a way to maintain relationships and to bolster interest in your community. They are also a highly effective and credible method to generate new leads. The goal for educational event marketing is the same as that of networking—to portray your organization as an involved community partner and a resource on the subject of senior living alternatives.

Many senior adults are curious about what retirement communities have to offer, but are reluctant to call or come in, thinking they'll get a "hard sell." Workshops and seminars offer a less threatening atmosphere for the market to learn more about your community, without the real or perceived pressure of listening to a sales presentation. Moreover, in the mind of the prospect, the notion of attending an educational program is more psychologically acceptable than the idea of looking at a retirement community as a potential future residence.

> Seminars are a great way to overcome the commonly encountered sales barrier of "I'm not ready yet."

Seminars are also a great way to overcome the commonly encountered sales barrier of "I'm not ready yet." If you think about it, your real competition isn't the community down the road, it's the consumer's own home; you must be more appealing than their cozy living room if you want to secure a sale. Featured speakers, which can include your residents, can offer information to senior consumers about the wisdom of planning for retirement living and show retirement housing as a superior alternative to remaining in their current home.

Or how about a seminar titled "Unlock the Equity Preserved in Your Home?" A panel of real estate and financial management presenters could provide strategies for converting senior adults' largest, most non-productive assets—their homes—into a more rewarding lifestyle, ranging from enjoying greater disposable income to the financial benefits of moving into a retirement community.

Not all of your seminars need to be on hard, head-spinning subjects. Why not host workshops or a series of do-it-yourself programs on topics such as gardening, painting, or cooking? For example, your foodservice staff can teach attendees how to whip up gourmet meals, to spotlight their expertise and your fine cuisine. And don't forget that residents are a sage source for sharing the how-to's of their varied hobbies and interests.

Through seminar marketing you can also reach and educate those who influence the prospect's decision. These decision influencers (as identified in your Strategic Networking Planner) have information needs different from the prospect, and your programming should be designed to meet their requirements as well. For example, you could host an educational program targeted to the adult child whose mom or dad is experiencing increasing needs and requires increasing support in order to remain at home. Promote the program with a provocative title that hits caregiver issues head-on, such as, "The Doctor Says He Checks Out Fine, But What About You?" Having a group of experts discuss the benefits of various wellness, health, and housing options, including your community, provides adult children with useful advice that can help direct their parent to the right resources.

Social Programs With a Purpose

Social events, such as holiday and anniversary celebrations, art shows, antique appraisals, luncheons, Sunday brunches, fashion shows, and open houses, are very popular among marketers and the market alike. From your standpoint, social events are somewhat easier to plan and execute than seminars. They're also a favorite with the "if-it's-free, it's-for-me" crowd who gather only long enough to eat your food and then waltz out the door.

Because of the festive tone, these programs can generate a lot of traffic. But don't let the big numbers fool you into thinking that the stampede can be counted on to generate qualified leads or help close the leads you already have. In this case, bigger is not better.

The goal of the social event is to draw a modest number of individuals so there is ample opportunity for quality interactions. Ours is a very information-intense product, and attendees won't learn about it by hearing your program in a crowded room or being herded through your community. And don't even think about selling through group tours and handing out reams of sales literature. Instead, structure your social programs so that you have smaller and more manageable groups. This way, attendees leave with a good understanding of the personality of your community and what you provide.

> Social events generate a lot of traffic, but don't let the big numbers fool you.

Some events, by their very nature, will draw large attendance (like a grand opening or anniversary celebration). You obviously don't want to discourage turnout by limiting attendance to these gala affairs. However, by hosting a large group, you must realize that motivating individuals to return for a personal presentation or tour will be challenging. They've been there. They've seen it. Their willingness to return anytime soon will be nominal at best. As an alternative, consider hosting a series of openings or celebrations for various groups: VIPs, residents, prospects, networking contacts, and the general public.

Imaginative Themes That Inspire Interest

Whether you're planning educational or social events, your topics should be creative, contemporary, and unbiased in tone so that you don't drive away the market with an overemphasis on aging or illness. Present upbeat topics that reinforce the positive aspects of growing older. Concentrate on programs that have universal appeal to any individual seeking to expand his or her knowledge and interests.

For inspiration, look at the educational and social calendars of area hospitals and colleges; all provide exceptional programming and promotions. Also examine the publications and Web sites of organizations or information purveyors who service the same target market that you do. For example, pick up a copy of the AARP publication, *The Magazine*, and you'll find stimulating articles and editorials on topics such as money, religion, health, travel, lifestyle, and family. Use these same subjects to introduce your special event and paid media campaigns. Instead of a seminar on "Bunions, Backaches, and Bursitis," how about "The Secrets of a 50-Year Marriage" where resident couples share serious and humorous insights on what it takes to make a long-term marriage work. Instead of entitling a health education program "Managing Diabetes," you could call it "Sweet Success—Managing Diabetes with Exercise and Diet." In Chapter 9, Creative Design and Copywriting, we'll cover the advertising images and phrases that have high market appeal and that can help to scrub our communities of the ageism that so often hampers the sales process.

> Host creative and contemporary programs—don't drive away the market with age-biased event themes.

Celebrity appearances are another way to impress the market with your "un-retiring" environment. They are most often associated with a big event, such as a grand opening or anniversary celebration. Celebrities can be national figures or local notables, prominent community leaders or politicians who would be a suitable addition to your big day. Radio and television talk show hosts and personalities also enjoy celebrity status and can draw a respectable crowd wherever they go. Before you become too enchanted with the idea of hobnobbing with a big name, think about whether this style of high-flying event marketing is right for your community and your area. In some locales, it's a popular and even expected promotional venue, whereas in other areas, the use of celebrities would be considered a bit over the top. Also consider what kind of personality or role model is most appropriate for your mission, image, and the impression you want to make.

Most communities host or participate in a variety of resident and community-related activities and festivities throughout the year. These include bake sales, blood drives, health fairs, wellness clinics, trade shows, and fund drives. Some communities also make their resident events and activities available for attendance by the general public (or selected prospects). While these programs go a long way toward fostering goodwill and are essential to being a good provider and community neighbor, they technically do not qualify as an authentic "special event."

> Special events are exclusively promoted to your wait-list, lead base, target market.

A distinction between resident relations, community relations, and event marketing is that a special event is a program that is exclusively and vigorously promoted to your wait-list, lead base, and target market. Keep this qualifier in mind as you plan your programs.

The Media Mix

Special events can be promoted through press releases, public service announcements, direct mail invitations, your newsletter, your Web site, newspaper, and even radio or television advertising. The promotional mix is determined by your intended target market and the nature of the event.

Before we look at how these various tools are used in event promotions, let's examine how you can extend your market reach for less cost by partnering with complementary businesses to co-host events. Area colleges, banks, hospitals, realtors, and law firms that you identified in your strategic networking endeavors are ideal cosponsors. They're often going after the same market you serve and are anxious to form alliances with experienced senior-adult service marketers. Be sure to investigate opportunities to promote the event in the cosponsor's marketing communication tools—their client list, organizational newsletters, and literature distribution points. This cross-marketing tactic enables you to introduce your community to the constituents of the cosponsoring organization, which may be an untapped market for you.

If you've done your media networking groundwork, now is the time to capitalize on those relationships. Send a press release or simple notification for inclusion in the media's listing of local happenings. Don't expect a feature story on the event unless you're hosting a particularly unique program or can present the event along with a human-interest story. Be sure to cover all forms of free press, which can include drive-by marquee signage, radio and television (cable), public service announcements (PSAs), and rack literature displays in permissible areas, from banks to beauty salons and health spas.

The real promotional power of event marketing is that it provides an outstanding opportunity for the inventive use of direct mail, print media, and electronic media. Many communities that use event-themed advertising report receiving more leads from their event ads than from the generic lifestyle ads that directly promote their community. It's no coincidence. The humdrum headlines of typical lifestyle ads (e.g., "Introducing Blue Sky Village…Retirement Living

FIGURE 3 Special Events Marketing Matrix

Strategy Frequency	Maintenance Biannually	Growth Quarterly
Target Markets	■ Wait-list ■ Lead base ■ Networking referral sources[1] ■ General market	■ Wait-list ■ Lead base ■ Networking referral sources[1] ■ Qualified market ■ General market
Promotional Methods	■ Press releases ■ Public service announcements ■ Phone calls to wait-list and lead base ■ Direct mail invitations, newsletters to wait-list and lead base ■ Minimal print media advertising (1-2 exposures) ■ Web site	■ Press releases ■ Public service announcements ■ Phone calls to wait-list and lead base ■ Direct mail invitations, newsletters to wait-list and lead base ■ Direct mail invitations and/or newsletters to rented list ■ Print media advertising (x4-6 exposures) ■ Web site

(1) Include (as appropriate) the primary and secondary focus markets identified in your Strategic Networking Planner.

at Its Best") are unoriginal and equally forgettable. Plus, this age-biased positioning typecasts a community as a "place for old people," and the market happens to be averse to any product or service that is designed for "old people." The goal is to attract, not repel, the market—and you accomplish this by portraying your community as a vibrant place to live, work, and learn.

This endorsement of paid media isn't a green light to proceed without a plan. Your event advertising approach must be deliberate and correlate to your marketing strategy. As discussed in Chapter 2, your analysis should have examined your marketing program's performance, paid advertising performance, and corresponding lead profiles. If you have this data, you essentially have your plan. Your future program becomes a repeat of the event frequency and promotional mix that worked for you in the past.

The Special Events Marketing Matrix

The Special Events Marketing Matrix (Figure 3) is for those communities that are new to event marketing or those communities that don't have the data to tailor their individual program. The Matrix demonstrates the frequency, target markets, and promotional methods for a maintenance and growth marketing strategy. It, along with the Special Events Planner in the *Marketing Plan Template*, provides a starting point for developing your own event promotions plan. Since the Matrix keys off maintenance and growth marketing strategies, let's revisit the definition of these two terms, first introduced in Chapter 2, before we get into its components.

> **A maintenance strategy** is called for when your community is at full occupancy (or at the occupancy goal) and you have a sufficient lead base and close rate to derive the targeted sales objective.
>
> **A growth strategy** is warranted for communities that are not operating at their assigned occupancy goal. To accomplish the goal, more sales need to be secured, either by increasing the close rate or by increasing the size of the lead base.

Notice that the Matrix target markets are similar for both maintenance and growth marketing strategies. You always want to work your markets from the inside out: begin with your wait list, then the lead base, networking referral sources, and finally the general market. A growth marketing strategy has the additional audience of age-and-income qualified market service area households. Let's explore tactics for promoting your events to each of these groups.

Calibrated Marketing

The primary difference between maintenance versus growth event-marketing strategies is in the event frequency and its promotional reach and intensity. If you're in a maintenance marketing mode, you'll want to host an event twice a year (biannually), which is all you really need since your assigned strategy reflects that you already have enough lead and sales activity to achieve your sales objective.

New communities, or those in a growth marketing mode, will need to increase the event frequency to at least once per quarter. In some extreme circumstances, such as a pre-marketing launch or occupancy-distressed community, a bimonthly frequency is employed for a short duration. You might also need a stepped-up schedule if you're hosting interrelated workshops, such as a "Lunch and Learn" series.

Now let's look at event advertising methods. In a maintenance marketing strategy, you would promote attendance from your wait-list and lead base through telephone invitations (made by the sales team), invitations mailed to the wait-list and lead base, and through cross-promotions on your Web site and in your newsletter, if your newsletter is designed as a high-quality communications tool. You also have the option of using newspaper advertising, but at a modest frequency of one or two exposures per event. In this case, print media is being used just to keep your name out there; any new leads or program attendance generated from these ads is an extra bonus.

If you're in a growth marketing mode you must take several additional steps. A growth strategy follows the same advertising grid, in that it will be promoted to your current lead base through phone calls, mailed invitations, newsletters, and postings on your Web site. However, in this case, you would also send invitations and/or your newsletter to a rented mailing list that contains the names of preselected age-and income-qualified individuals in your market area (discussed in Chapter 12).

Since your goal is to generate more leads, you would also employ more intensive newspaper advertising, with a range of four to six exposures per event or as the schedule allows. You can supplement your promotions with electronic media, but limit its use to momentous events, like a grand opening. The rules on event crowd control still apply, so keep in mind that when you use these media (radio and television) you're really losing control over who and how many individuals turn out to trample your shiny new community.

Communication Integration

When it comes to the design and production of your promotional materials, remember that the process isn't about cranking out stand-alone mailers and ads. The goal is to ensure that all promotional materials are integrated—their overall appearance, tone, and content should be the same. Designing all promotional components to work together as a unified force rather than each working in isolation is the essence of integrated marketing communications. Here's an overview of how to synchronize your media to supplement one another.

The only way that integrated marketing communication can occur is if you have a game plan for each promotional component and a vision for how it ties into the whole program. For your networking, event, and paid media programs to interlock, you must know your event timing, topics, intended audiences, and promotional methods for the entire year. As you network, you should be alert for opportunities to partner with complementary businesses in joint programming. When you're developing your newsletters and ads, your topics should be somewhat predefined and written to echo the event themes. If you know what's ahead, you can expediently convert a lifestyle ad into an event ad just by adding a banner or "snipe" announcement.

> All promotional materials should have integrated content and unified visuals.

Having a plan also makes it easy to say "no" to all the pesky vendors who contact you for advertising placement in their "oh-so-special, one-of-a-kind" senior directory because you already know where your investment is being directed. The Special Events Planner in the *Marketing Plan Template* will help you achieve this level of event choreography and integration.

Advertising Appeal

Your newsletter is going to do the lion's share of promotional work so you'll want to make sure it's designed as a high-quality direct mailer. Be sure to include newsworthy articles of interest to the target market, particularly topics that tie into the featured event theme.

Let's say you're planning a program titled "Making the Move," a seminar on how to prepare for a lifestyle change. You intend to feature financial planners, realtors, moving professionals, and interior decorators who will offer advice to attendees on how to minimize the headaches of moving from their present residence to a new home. A companion newsletter article (perhaps contributed by the featured financial planner) could discuss the economic advantages of downsizing from a large home to a smaller residence. Or, the realtor could submit an article on how to get a house in market-ready condition.

The newsletter should always contain a reply coupon that offers the option to register or RSVP for the program, which for some consumers is a preferred contact method as opposed to a phone call.

The same design and copy is then used in your newspaper ad. It should address the theme and notable speakers (if applicable), include your phone number, and instructions for registration or RSVP. The ad should also contain a reply coupon to provide the reader a choice of either attending the event or receiving more information about your community.

Every ad should be anchored with a brief narrative or descriptive tag line that describes who and what you are and a "call to action" that explains what you want the reader to do. A succinct and appealing positioning statement and call to action might be something like, "…a collection of homes and services designed to meet your needs now and in years to come….call today to learn more!"

Begin your newspaper advertising, using the same ad, three weeks before the event for a maintenance strategy, and four weeks in advance for a growth strategy. Your event invitations are a visual knockoff of the newspaper ad (sans the reply coupon).

If you're having trouble conceptualizing these creative concepts, don't worry about it right now. You'll learn a lot more about integrated marketing communications in the next few chapters.

The Day of the Show

When it comes to event execution, all programs need to be carefully staged and key staff need to be included in the process. Begin to solidify individual event plans about three months out to allow ample time for promotional and day-of-the-event logistics execution.

Think through the entire agenda, from the first registration phone call to when the last guest leaves. Prepare a script for the reception staff to use to make sure you capture the names and contact information of individuals who call to RSVP. Use a guest registration book or raffle to obtain attendee contact information once they're on-site. The attendee list is later used to identify new leads for the sales team to court through telephone and direct mail follow up.

Think about event parking and access, primary greeters, traffic flow, seating, refreshments, fresh flowers, and entertainment. Determine exactly what community information will be provided and how it will be furnished. Never, never, never hand out your entire information brochure, floor plans, and prices. Avoid providing group tours and instead determine how you'll flag interested individuals and get them back for a personal presentation.

During the event, don't let a few noisy and nosy prospects monopolize your time. This is your show, which means it's no time for the hostess to be holed up in her office with a prospect. Have your appointment book handy so you can politely suggest a private session.

When it's all over, sit down with your team to review the program. What worked and what needs to be fine-tuned? Which vendors and presenters would you use again? Was the attendee feedback positive? Given all that went into staging the program, was it worth doing? What is the sales plan of attack for new individuals who expressed interest and old prospects who need a nudge?

So far we have covered the first two elements of your promotional plan: networking and special events. Now that the foundation has been laid, let's move into those critical components that comprise the advertising portion of your marketing program: Creative design and copywriting, collateral materials, direct mail, print media, and electronic media.

> It's hard to imagine anyone getting too excited over the notion of moving into a "facility" or being thrilled at the idea of living in a "studio unit."

9

Creative Design And Copywriting—What To Say And Portray

Creative design and copywriting are terms that refer to the images and words used in your marketing communication materials. You may be familiar with the advertising agency lingo of "graphic design" and "copy." The visuals and text of your advertising materials must be carefully crafted to help the market see exactly what you want them to see—a concept that our industry has not found easy to execute.

Despite the fact that our marketing machines have been hard at work informing and educating the consumer for more than three decades, our communities are still perceived as a "last resort" or as "old folks' homes" by the majority of the market. Prospects often remind us that they are too young or "not ready" to move to our kind of place. Unfortunately, our marketing communication materials, with their use of age-biased phrases such as "retirement community," photographs of "old people," and institutional-sounding copy, perpetuate the very image our market seeks to avoid. It's hard to imagine anyone getting too excited over the notion of moving into a "facility" or being thrilled at the idea of living in a "studio unit."

This chapter explores alternative creative design and copywriting concepts that have maximum market appeal. The fundamentals are covered here; the mechanical execution of these concepts is detailed in the upcoming chapters.

Crafting the Right Message

Look at your marketing communication materials as well as those of other communities. Traditionally, most place a heavy emphasis on services, such as meals, housekeeping, maintenance, activities, and transportation. If you think about it, this emphasis throws up several sales barriers. Some senior consumers are repelled by a service-rich environment—not because they don't find the concept appealing at some level, but because they still consider themselves independent and are resistant to the notion of living in a retirement community. Most often these services are communicated using a sterile copy format, such as bulleted line listings. Prospects then whip through your selling points and conclude they don't need, and don't want to pay for, all the services you offer. It's no wonder so many prospects tell us, "I'm shopping for the future…for when I need your services."

Compelling Copy

You're probably asking, what do you write about if you're not to get into the details of your meals, housekeeping, transportation, and activities? The better question is, what should you discuss first?

Your advertising copy needs to respond to the interests and concerns of the senior consumer, and your target market in particular, which are most likely similar. Surveys tell us that a common attribute of many senior adults is that they own their homes free and clear, and that their homes are their primary financial asset. However, they also report having difficulty with home maintenance—from a number of perspectives. Household upkeep and taxes pose a financial burden, utility costs are too high and continue to rise, and finding reliable and reputable household labor is difficult. Because of soaring property taxes, insurance, maintenance, and utility costs, many senior adults find themselves today in the predicament of being "house rich and cash poor." Your target market may have substantial home equity, but monthly expenses can consume as much as one-half their income.

> The selling point of "two daily meals and weekly housekeeping" is dull and falls on deaf ears.

While this information is hardly news, what is remarkable is that we don't capitalize on this consumer profile in our advertising messages. Instead, we base our primary selling points on "…two daily meals and weekly housekeeping" and the peace of mind and security that living in a retirement community can bring. It's a rather dull and funereal message that is falling on deaf ears.

Rather than dwell on the "three hots and a cot" message (which makes for grim reading and does nothing to distinguish you from your competitor, who is sending the same message in the same way), you need to cast your community as an attractive and affordable alternative to home upkeep. Your copy should be compelling enough to draw the reader in and make it easy for him to get the message. Tell your customers a story about the life they can expect and how it's made possible by the services and amenities that you offer.

For example, "Over the years you've cared for your family and others, doing what needed to be done. Now is the time to make good on the promises you made to yourself years ago—to enjoy an uncomplicated, yet full lifestyle. Our cottages and apartment homes are a welcome alternative to the headaches of heating and cooling unused rooms, yard work, and the endless chores of home maintenance and upkeep."

Additional marketing messages that appeal to senior consumers are those of life-enriching social programs (and we're not talking about Bingo), educational opportunities, and community involvement. In other words, present a way of life, not just a generic service package.

> Once you have created your compelling message, don't kill your Kodak moment with geriatric words and phrases.

Once you have created your compelling message, don't kill your Kodak moment with geriatric words and phrases. Nothing says "old" faster than "senior citizen," "retiree," "elderly," "aged," or cliché euphemisms like "leisure years" and "golden years." If you must define who it is you are designed to serve, which isn't necessary with the right copy and casting, then use "mature adult" or "senior adult."

Similarly, think about the words and phrases you use to describe your product. Many mature communities struggle with the appearance of a dated physical plant and the shortcomings of smaller units. That doesn't mean, however, that your sales and advertising copy needs to be equally antiquated and riddled with words that amplify these limitations. Dated and institutional-sounding terms include "facility," "building," "rooms," "unit," "campus," "wing," "center," "one- and two-room efficiencies," and "kitchenettes." This industry jargon is fine when we're speaking to each other, but it is a dreadful depiction of a place to call home. Would you want to tell your friends that you live in a "one-bedroom unit on the south-wing?" And if you think about it, you don't hear residents using these terms either. Instead, discuss your "residence," "community," and your "apartments" or "apartment homes." With a little imagination and wordplay, you can turn those studio units that feature a kitchenette into "comfortable accommodations with an efficient kitchen."

If your community offers a continuum of care or other forms of healthcare, you'll need to be careful in how you portray these settings and services as well.

Keep in mind that in this situation, your message is being read by the adult child as well as the senior consumer. While the terms that we use to describe independent living, assisted living, dementia care, and skilled care are a fast way to sum up your services when speaking to other providers, such language can read a bit bleak if not artfully addressed in your copy. We all know that consumers who select a continuing care retirement community (or one that offers a continuum of service) do so because of the availability of these programs. However, that does not mean they want to be whacked over the head with sterile, institutional jargon that points to their impending, and most likely final, destination place.

> If your community offers a continuum of care, you'll need to be careful in how you portray these settings and services.

For example, the phrase "independent living" is a popular senior-housing descriptor. But what exactly does that mean anyway? Does it mean a person isn't independent if she doesn't live in an "independent living" retirement community? Or, if a person resides in "assisted living" does that mean he's no longer an independent individual? And who wants to live in a dementia unit?

As an alternative to care-level labels, strive to conceive a collection of tasteful program names developed around a central theme associated with your community name. Or you can use the name of a person or place—there are no set rules. An appealing name draws the reader into the body copy that does the work—describing what the program does and the needs it fulfills.

Since we're on the subject of names, let's get down to a basic issue that has challenged our industry for years: should you use the terms "retirement" or "retirement community" as part of your community name? The answer is no, if you can avoid it. As we learn more about senior consumers and their dislike for age-biased products, we now know that it's a good idea to distance your community from names or descriptors that conjure up the image of an "old folks' home."

If you're a project in the planning stages, arriving at an "age-free" name is a problem-free process. However, putting a new twist on an established name is not so easy, and without careful planning, such a move can spell an iconoclastic disaster. In these situations, the advantages of a name change or modification need to be carefully weighed against the cost of potentially disenfranchising the very market that is the reason for your existence. Your name could stand for years of history and tradition. It may be synonymous with a heritage of caring for older adults. Or you may be a religiously affiliated community that depends on the support of your key constituents.

If you decide to pursue a name change or modification, you'll need to be very cautious, do your research, foster ideas and support from your stakeholders, and have a thorough game plan for how and when you will introduce your new identity to your various audiences.

Create a Commotion With Graphic Emotion

Creative marketing communication materials always include graphic elements that work to add interest and allure, and help to sell the product. Typeface and style and the use of color, images of people, places, objects, and situations all serve to enhance and dramatize your words.

When it comes to graphic design, we should take lessons from the retail product and service industries—they know that good design is all about emotion and what the product will allow the customer to achieve. There is less emphasis on the product itself and more on what the product will do. Emotion-laced advertising creates an image that represents what people want or hope to be.

To determine if your present materials meet the "emotional mark" of good graphic execution, gather your collateral materials and ads, as well as the materials of half-a-dozen other communities. Spread them out on a table and absorb the overall impression. You will likely find a common graphic direction that revolves around one or more of the following three themes: pictures of the building (inside and out), pictures of residents (or models posing as residents), and illustrations or photos that depict familiar references. Let's analyze the real-estate angle first.

> Good graphic design is all about emotion and what the product will allow the customer to achieve.

You have to admit, there is nothing particularly creative about slapping a picture of a building onto the cover of a brochure. Sure, it's a great way to fill space, and the architects and owners are rightly proud of the building's design, but does this visual image really express to the market that the featured community is a place where life is a celebration? The visual is what it is—a picture of a building.

Now take a look at the predictable photos of apartments and amenity areas. Do these images conjure any emotions other than perhaps "that's nice?" Remember that your number-one competitor is the prospect's current home. Do you honestly think that the dressed-up apartment shot or the wide-angle dining room photo can stand up to the home they have lived in for years? So why put the visual emphasis on the real estate when you can't even begin to compete in that arena?

Some of you may be shaking your heads in disagreement and thinking of dozens of residents that just love, love, love the appearance of your community, its design, the apartments, and all the amenities it offers. Great—your market finds you attractive. Well, let's hope so. But was it the appearance of your community that compelled them to move? It's doubtful.

Now let's assess the second graphic approach—that of depicting residents or models generally having the time of their lives digging in the garden, eating in the dining room, stretching in the wellness room, tossing back a toddy in the lounge, or Web surfing in the computer lab. There's nothing wrong with this pictorial approach, if you show the right people in the right setting, with exceptional professional photography and graphic execution.

Take the affordable approach, shooting the photos yourself, and the end product can come off as amateurish or unappealing—especially if your photographs are of the grainy black-and-white variety typically seen in ads and newsletters.

The use of models (whether custom or stock photography) carries with it the danger of creating an invented world that is more fantasy than fact. You run the risk of individuals being a bit surprised when they see your actual resident profile or learn that the handsome couple featured on the inside cover of your brochure really doesn't live at your community.

> An ad that shows a senior adult rollerblading may be hip and clever, but it's absurd when you consider how most prospects spend their time.

Speaking of fantasy, you also want to be careful about portraying residents in contrived roles. An ad that shows a senior adult rollerblading or mountain biking may be hip and clever, but it's also absurd when you consider how most prospects spend their time. You may be able to defend this tactic with the contention that you are preparing for the next demographic wave of senior consumers, the silent and boomer generations. Or you may have a few residents who actually do start their day with a five-mile run instead of a morning stroll. If you want to cast these resident exceptions as a representation of your market, or break new ground with "pioneering" creative concepts that target a previously untapped market—then go ahead: It's your money.

How to Cast Your Community

Contrary to popular practice, your printed materials don't need to feature photos of your product or your patrons to say that you're a community that serves older adults. This premise takes us into the final and perhaps most flexible graphic theme: the use of a blend of images and visual references that universally appeals to senior adults on an emotionally stimulating level. These are poignant and provocative images (typically associated with the benefits of the product) that subtly suggest or reference the possibilities, both familiar and new, that await the consumer. These can include:

- Images that say, "this is your home," such as a comfortable chair, a welcome mat, a quilt, a good book, or any familiar or cherished possession. Think of the paintings of Norman Rockwell or Thomas Kincaid, which represent all that is good about home. Try to create the same emotional tug.

- Nature scenes, such as gardens, water, woods, birds, and flowers.

- Images of health, wellness, and fitness, including nutritious food, a pair of walking shoes, or a set of dumbbells or other appropriate sports equipment.
- Suggestions of travel, such as train, airline, or cruise tickets.
- Symbols of culture, self-learning, and education, which can include books, a fine writing pen or a writing desk, or theater tickets.
- Nostalgic depictions and themes, vintage family photos, for example, have an appeal that cuts across all generations—both the market we serve today and the generations of the future. Society's preoccupation with time-saving technology and conveniences has made nostalgic messages increasingly popular because they recall a simpler, happier time.

These timeless icons can be used alone, as the basis of your entire graphic approach, or in combination with images of your community and its residents.

The Lowdown on Branding

This chapter wouldn't be complete without a reference to the subject of branding or brand advertising. Just for the record, a brand is the symbolic embodiment of all the information connected with a product or service. A brand typically includes a name, a logo, a tag line (or slogan), and accompanying visual images or symbols. Ideally, a brand is supposed to set up the market's expectations about a particular product or service. When the brand name is used, it is supposed to elicit product recall.

True brand advertising is highly involved, expensive, and complex. Brand concepts include the "brand experience," which is the sum experience of all points of contact with the product. When a brand is widely known in the marketplace, it has achieved "brand recognition." When there is a mass positive experience with a product, it has achieved "brand franchise." "Brand equity" is the extent of the franchise.

If you consider this textbook definition of branding and brand constructs, you'll probably agree that as an industry we have a long way to go before our communities become household names like Hershey, Coca-Cola, or Kleenex. Branding is certainly not a critical marketing component at this point; we're still struggling with the rudiments of what to call ourselves and how to best explain and depict our programs and services. It will be quite some time, if ever, before the phrase "retirement community" becomes a household word.

> It will be quite some time, if ever, before the phrase "retirement community" becomes a household word.

So don't get hoodwinked with ad agency tomfoolery that attempts to push you into a brand campaign, or that passes off nothing more than clever slogans and slick brochures as brand advertising. Your immediate marketing communications goal is to establish a compelling message and an appealing portrayal of your community that banish old age stereotypes. Communicating a recurrent theme that is visually consistent is essential. This discussion may sound a lot like brand advertising, but it's not about branding, it's about arriving at a good design.

If you have advanced your marketing program to the point where it is time to undertake a legitimate brand campaign, you still need to assess the operational world around you to make sure your community is firing on all cylinders and that you have a clear strategic plan that identifies your organization's future direction and destination.

When collateral materials are produced by anyone other than an experienced graphic designer, they rarely have the pizzazz that motivates older adults to read and keep them.

10
Collateral Materials—Print Communications That Pack A Punch

This critical marketing component plays a big role in the world of marketing communications. A well-designed collateral package is a highly effective sales tool, providing your team with a way to customize how and when information is presented to prospects. It's also an effective consumer-decision aid, allowing prospects the opportunity to absorb information at their own pace and to retain your materials for future reference.

This chapter explores the role, use, and mechanical design specifications for the primary elements of your collateral package, which includes everything from your information brochure to your application and contract documents. Another way to think of the collateral family is that it consists of any printed material that is used for marketing and sales communications.

Before we move into specifics, let's first review your role in the creative design and production process of these materials. In terms of glamour and appeal, collateral materials are a favorite among marketers. The time spent running around taking pictures for your next newsletter is a wonderful distraction from the mission-critical work of filling your building. There's nothing like the big splash of a glossy new brochure to showcase your creative genius and your ability to deliver the community's collateral materials, all by yourself, on a modest budget.

This facetious description of how most collateral materials come about is meant to illustrate that while a homegrown design may save you some money, it also costs valuable time. It will also cost you leads. When collateral materials are produced by anyone other than a trained and experienced art director or graphic designer, they rarely have the graphic pizzazz that motivates older adults to read and keep them. Let's be brutally honest: Unless you're that rare breed who knows how to turnkey an integrated marketing program and expertly design and produce collateral materials—you're not the right person to be writing, designing, and producing your print communication materials. And that's okay—in fact, it's preferred. Your marketing role is to create and orchestrate the game plan for how your entire collaterals package will play out, from the types of materials needed to support your total marketing program, to how the materials should be physically fashioned to achieve economies and visual cohesion. You then work with an industry-specialized ad agency or graphics firm that turns out the work you have outlined.

Let's begin your plan right now, by reviewing the specifications for a standard collateral package that consists of:

- Primary information brochure
- Introductory or overview brochure
- Brochure inserts, such as floor plans, a services and amenity listing, application and contract documents
- Stationery package
- Marketing newsletter
- CD or DVD

Primary Information Brochure

Think of your marketing literature as a montage of materials that serve individual purposes and at the same time come together to form a visually cohesive communications brief. The information brochure is the anchor for the entire package. It sets the creative tenor for all subsequent materials and is responsible for communicating most of the information on your community's concept, services, and amenities. Since we've already reviewed the essentials of creative design and copywriting in Chapter 9, let's discuss the brochure's mechanical specifications—how it should be physically structured in shape and style to meet with market favor.

Design Specifications

Let's first review some guidelines for the brochure's size. This is one area where ad agencies like to be clever—they'll try selling you on a teeny-weeny cute brochure or an oversized monster. But in the end, practicality wins. It's better to let the brochure's design be memorable in other ways. Instead of pursuing some off-the-wall size, stay with the tried and true 9" wide x 12" tall format. It tests well with the market (because it's standard and familiar), and it's affordable to produce, print, and mail in stock catalog envelopes. The biggest benefit is that the 9" x 12" size accommodates all the 8.5" x 11" inserts that you need to support your sales efforts, from correspondence to floor plans and contract documents.

However, we're not talking about the basic and boring 9" x 12" pocket folder that contains a lot of loose inserts. While this format allows you to update information quickly and inexpensively, that is exactly the message that it sends to the market. It's a cheap design treatment and it looks cheap. The information is subject to change, and senior consumers dread change. The irony is obvious: Here you are promising consumers a high-quality program and you are making this promise on low-quality collaterals.

> The quality of your collateral materials must be on par with your contention that you're a quality community.

The quality of your materials must be on par with your contention that you are a superior community that offers superior services and programs. This quality is expressed in part by the brochure's format. Instead of using inserts to tell your story, provide this information on pages that are stitched or affixed (known as "saddle-stitching") into a pocketed folder. With this format, you're looking at an eight-page brochure: the front and back covers, plus two inside pages. Just so you know, printers always count each side of the paper as one page.

The use of three or more colors in the base design theme is sufficient to create visual interest. However, you can really add impact with four-color processing without adding a lot more cost. What drives up job costs are what printers refer to as the "finish work," such as uncommon paper stock, odd-sizing, flaps, foils, and embossing.

While we're on the subject of color, keep in mind that your readers are older adults. Their eyes perceive primary colors better than pastels. Legibility is also important. Use a basic black, easy-to-read minimum 12-point typeface; avoid using all italics, all capital letters, underlined type, and reversed lettering.

Paper stock also influences readability and even the reader's emotional response. You'll want to invest in a substantial stock that has a high-quality look and feel. A better paper will be more expensive, but you can economize on the back end of the process by using a less expensive paper stock with your ancillary collateral materials.

Also think about the finish of the paper. For example, glossy white stock is a great backdrop for color photography and is frequently used in corporate brochures. However, it also makes type difficult to read, and at a subliminal level it may be incongruous with your intended warm message that says, "This is your home."

As least one pocket should contain a slit, also known as a "die-cut," to hold a business card. It's also a good idea to include a locator map on the brochure's back cover, or on the inside pocket panel, along with a call to action to obtain more information. And don't forget, your brochure, and all your print communication materials for that matter, should contain the organization's logo, slogan or tag line, name, address, phone number, Web site address, an Equal Housing Opportunity statement, and any special accreditations that your community has received.

The Graphic Portfolio

Every aspect of your collateral package, from the information brochure to your newsletter and note cards, must be consistent in design, colors used, and graphic elements employed. This consistency, or visual integration, establishes a look that the market will immediately associate with your community. This look is also known as a graphic "signature." This signature is achieved by determining: 1) the visuals that you will use in all pieces, and 2) what information is to be contained within each piece. This advance planning must precede the production phase of your collaterals.

As marketing director, you need to identify, or at least have some firm ideas on, the themes you intend to use. Be sure to work with your stakeholders, residents, and even your prospects to affirm your direction. However, don't fall into the trap of "designing by committee." Maintain control over the design process and remember, in the end, you know what images and messages will appeal to your market. Your visual references can be photos and/or illustrations of people, places, subjects, or scenes. Ideally, there should be a "creative rationale" for their use and an association with your target market profile and the lifestyle you offer.

Next, invest in the creative design and production of a collection of these images or vignettes. These will become your graphic portfolio, and some or all of the visuals that are initially introduced in your information brochure will be used repeatedly in the balance of your print communication materials, such as your smaller introductory brochure, postcards, newsletters, and newspaper ads. This knockoff method of design establishes strong market recall while providing a highly efficient and very cost-effective method of producing all the print communication materials that are required by the marketing program.

A popular graphic direction is the use of "stock photos" that can be purchased from various photo publishing companies. The advantage of this graphic direction is that you can obtain professional photos without the cost of custom photography. The disadvantage of stock photography is that its use has become so prolific that it's common to see multiple senior housing collaterals and ads (often in the same market), featuring the same photos.

A practical approach is to establish your graphic portfolio by using first-generation graphic design (illustrations and/or photos) and supplement with the sparing use of stock photography. Should you choose to develop your own library of customized photographs, be certain to use an experienced photographer; we're not talking about a portrait or wedding photographer either. As the "director" of your photo shoot, you must carefully orchestrate each frame, from the models' attire to the props and settings used. Dress your cast in solid primary-colored clothing—no plaids, prints or floral—and spend the extra money to have a makeup artist on hand.

Pacing Information Through Inserts

Primarily, collateral materials are intended to inspire interest and inform and educate the customer about your offerings. However, collateral materials do not sell your community. Your collateral materials are an extension of your sales effort, not a replacement. That's why they're called "collateral" materials.

Printed sales literature is meant to accompany and support expert sales practices. Your copy placement (and information pacing) must respect this basic premise. Use the inside pages of your information brochure to acquaint the reader with what you have to offer. The discussion should be on timeless subject matter that is relevant to what most readers would want to know. You don't want the copy to be so information-dense that it "gives away the farm."

> Collateral materials are an extension of your sales effort, not a replacement. That's why they're called "collateral" materials.

This approach is not a recommendation to avoid providing prospects with the details they need and want to know. Rather, it's about how and when to provide the details. The overview furnished in the brochure or other printed material provides an engaging preview intended to arouse the prospect's interest. Through relationship building and discovery, the sales representative learns what's important and appealing to the prospect. Detailed information on your community is relegated to inserts, so you can customize both the amount and type of information you provide to the prospect. This design format simply mirrors good sales practices by avoiding canned recitations.

Your graphic treatment of these materials is just as important as your copy approach—this is no hodgepodge of photocopies that clearly look as if they were an afterthought.

Avoid the common presentation method of "staircase" inserts, which are sheets of paper that have been cut to stack up at various heights. These materials need to be produced on full-sized 8.5" x 11" paper stock, or larger.

Elements of the creative signature established in your information brochure, which can include your logo, paper stock, and visuals, should be carried over onto your inserts. At the very least, make sure you have continuity in type fonts and colors.

If you go the distance in your graphic treatment of these materials, you can turn your inserts into dynamic sales aids. Let's look at some insert examples to understand how.

Floor Plans

Floor plans are a popular sales tool but they can turn into a sales barrier if not properly produced. For example, it's a mistake to put multiple floor plans on one page, or render them in a reduced, scale-less size. Why would you want to make your apartments appear smaller than they already are? Are you trying to save on your paper and postage costs? Is this the format someone handed you and told you to use? Or, do you think tiny gives a tidier appearance? Why would you want to introduce customers to a confusing array of floor plans that can be either too expensive or too small, when they will select only one?

> Never use second-generation photocopies of your floor plans, or any other insert for that matter.

Try this tactic instead: Put just one floor plan per page, and design the floor plan to a referenced scale, a minimum of at least one-quarter-inch to the foot. Depict and label the location of phone, TV, and electrical outlets, as well as linen, and coat closets, and all appliances. Report individual room sizes, but consider not reporting total square footage—no sense in drawing attention to the fact that your apartments can't rival the space found in a prospect's home. It's also a good idea to have a disclaimer on your floor plans that the reported room dimensions and features may vary; this is especially important for projects that are pre-marketing and the actual product has not been built.

Never use second-generation photocopies of your floor plans, or any other insert for that matter. Remember that at some point, prospects are going to learn about your monthly service fees and they will most likely think your pricing is too high, or more than they can afford. You don't want them holding a tired, faded photocopy of a floor plan in their hand when they do. Now you may argue that the customer is buying "security, comfort, and peace of mind," so why all the fuss about the need to provide pretty, printed floor plans? Well, for what consumers are paying, they should have the best.

A great way to augment the appearance and practicality of your floor plans is to design them as 17" x 11" inserts, that fold down to 8.5" x 11". This format provides room for narrative copy on standard apartment features, an area for the prospect to make notes, or for you to enumerate the fee(s) associated with the home or apartment under consideration.

Services and Amenities Listing

This insert provides a detailed description of the community's services and amenities that are included in the entry and/or monthly service fee. As with your floor plans, it can be designed to include an area to record notes, or for you to specify the fee range, or fees associated with a particular apartment.

Application and Contract Documents

Ironically, when consumers first inquire, they are often handed a decent looking brochure, but as they grow closer to residency, they are presented with an ever-increasing and unattractive array of forms to be filled out and processed. A contract signing is a reason to celebrate, so make this important occasion memorable for all the right reasons.

Think of your application and contract documents as the final chapter of your information inserts. These documents should be presented on good stationery, in a professional and standardized format, and designed with an eye toward eliminating redundant information.

Price Sheets

While price sheets, or fee schedules, are presented here as a potential insert, they really shouldn't be an insert at all—at least by themselves. In fact, price sheets that make public every price for every unit type, without the accompanying communication of the benefits received, top the list of big marketing blunders. True, most marketers use this method to relay community pricing information. However, if you think about it, this sales tradition only amplifies a common marketing barrier, namely the perception that the prospect cannot afford your community.

The defensive chorus for this prevalent practice goes something like this: "Consumers demand to know our prices, and that demand begins with the first phone call. They don't want to come in, they don't want to hear a sales presentation, and some don't even want to be mailed a brochure. They are just shopping around and they want to know how much we cost. Besides, they have just checked with several other communities before calling us, all of whom willingly revealed their fees. If we don't provide the requested information, we'll lose them. So we give callers the pricing information they want."

This quick surrender is a sure sign of undeveloped sales skills—or it indicates that the sales representative has become just plain lazy. A professional knows how to take control of the call and put the focus where it belongs: meeting the prospect's needs. This isn't achieved by robotically reciting apartment pricing and mailing out a brochure that is jam-packed with information on entry fees, monthly fees, application fees, and reservation fees.

Your fees should never be printed on a single insert that contains nothing but your pricing grid. Prospects have already been set back by the shock of your high prices, so why compound the situation further with the frustration that comes with having to tunnel their way through your literature to ascertain what services they receive in relation to price? Instead, the objective is to communicate value along with your price. Here's how.

> Pricing information should always be conveyed in conjunction with a value.

Your verbal and written presentation tempo should always align with prospects' orientation and interest in retirement housing in general, and with your community in particular. If you overload your prospects by phone or by mail, you rob yourself of the opportunity to get them in for a personal presentation. A prospect's reaction is to back off and give you the dreaded "I'm not ready yet" response. When explaining your fees over the phone or in person, you should quote a price range, a beginning price point, or the fee for a particular unit type (the prospect's unit of interest). Thereafter, you can communicate this same information in writing, using either your floor plans or your services and amenities insert designed as specified.

Of course, this process means that you must understand the prospect's profile before you provide pricing information. Competent sales representatives always put profile before price.

Introductory Brochures

This smaller version of your primary information brochure has multiple uses. Sometimes referred to as a "trifold brochure" or "#10 brochure" (because it is sized to fit in a standard letter envelope), the introductory brochure can be developed as an overview of your total community, or as literature that promotes a particular program or care level.

Introductory brochures are a low-cost information primer for initial inquirers who won't spend the time for you to determine if your community is right for their needs. They can also be used for mass distribution, whether as a direct mailer to your target markets, literature for rack displays, or leave-behind materials when you make networking visits.

If you've already established a look for your primary information brochure, your introductory brochure is easy to produce. You simply lift selected copy and visuals, and design it as a trifold that includes a reply card for the respondent to obtain more information. It's also smart to devise the brochure as a stand-alone direct mailer. Be sure to include the necessary postage indicia and return address information on the reply coupon. Chapter 12, Direct Mail, details these and other design specifications.

Stationery Package

It should be obvious by now that your stationery package (letterhead, envelope, and business card) needs to visually marry with the information brochure. Strive to make an impact with its appearance and don't compromise your look to save a few dollars. For example, the envelopes you use to mail your information brochure should be just as distinctive as the piece itself, so it's a good idea to invest in either a graphically designed, custom-sized envelope, or use a stock envelope with a custom mail label. This may seem like a frivolous expense if you're on a tight budget, but think about the potential return. You want customers to feel excited when they reach into the mailbox to retrieve your materials, and the standard institutional-tan mailing envelope and Avery mail label just doesn't do the job.

Remember, for our market, letter writing was at one time their primary means of communication. For some, it was and still is a fine art to be pursued with a favorite writing instrument and personal stationery selection. That's why it's a good idea to produce graphically matching note cards as part of your stationery package. People love to receive a penned note. Note cards are an ideal enclosure for your information brochure because they're fast yet personal. They can also be used in lieu of a potentially unwelcome phone call to touch base with a customer you've been working with for some time.

The Marketing Newsletter

A marketing newsletter has numerous uses, and as such, it can be classed as either a collateral piece or a direct mail device. Whatever the classification, the multiple benefits of the newsletter are clear. A newsletter functions as a steady market reminder of your presence. It establishes and enhances your organization's credibility. Through the information you provide, the market becomes attuned to the quality of your services and the satisfaction of those you serve. Best of all, a newsletter allows you to shape the way your community is viewed. In its pages you can play up your strengths, call attention to your accomplishments, and communicate your message in a way that prompts readers to develop a positive impression and an interest in your community.

These benefits may sound similar to those of the information brochure. However, there is one principal difference: The brochure content is static, while your newsletter content is fluid and can be manipulated to meet the requirements of the marketing communications program.

The collateral newsletter should not be confused with the in-house newsletter that is geared toward, and sometimes published by, residents. Also referred to as a marketing newsletter, the collateral newsletter's content and design is exclusively geared toward the external market.

Every issue should contain a cover story about a subject of global interest to senior consumers, such as health, money management, religion, travel, or family. This feature story is complemented by an article that spotlights a community offering. Ideally, the two articles should interrelate—for example, you could feature an article on "health and wellness" as a lead into showcasing your community's wellness program.

Now, go one step further and use your newsletter to promote the upcoming event that you have planned on the same subject. If you have completed the Special Events Planner in the *Marketing Plan Template*, you already have a major portion of your newsletter content outlined for the year. Supplement this content with a message from management, resident profiles, testimonials, or a new resident welcome column. You can also feature your monthly calendar of events and festivities. Just remember, we're not talking about the typical activities calendar that reads like a preschoolers' program.

> Avoid resident memorials, staff announcements, and fund solicitation subject matter.

Be sure to present resident profiles in an upbeat manner. Too often, resident profiles can backfire, because of unattractive photography or residents who cite health problems or the loss of a spouse as reasons for moving. Although these may be some of the very reasons consumers join a retirement community, most prospects don't want to be reminded of their tenuous situation.

While we're on the topic of sensitive subject matter, let's talk about a few more "topic-traps" to avoid. Remember to sidestep any ageist and poor-health-related themes. Instead of a cover story on "preventing falls," put a health and wellness spin on it and tuck the helpful fall-prevention information inside the newsletter. Definitely avoid resident memorials or using your marketing newsletter for fund development and fund solicitation. Staff announcements is another subject that does not have a place in this newsletter. Although it's important to recognize and welcome new staff, this kind of information holds little value or interest for a general market—unless of course you live in a very small town where one-third of the town is employed at your community. Repeated staff announcements can also draw attention to a turnover problem that your community may be experiencing.

Your collateral newsletter needs to have a professional, appealing design and a consistent visual theme. Photographs and/or illustrations consistent with your information brochure should be employed throughout. Use colors that are common to the rest of your collateral materials, usually two-color, and even up to four-color processing. The newsletter should be at least four pages in length (17" x 11" folded down to 8.5" x 11") and designed as a self-mailer with a perforated reply coupon to accommodate use in your direct mail campaigns. In determining content volume, be sure to leave room for visuals and direct mail postage requirements. For example, you'll need about a half page to feature your upcoming event. The same copy and graphics can be repeated in companion event invitations and newspaper ads.

This marketing synergy can only be accomplished if you have planned each issue's frequency and content at the front-end of your marketing process and in conjunction with your special events, direct mail, and print media advertising schedule. Remember that your event frequency is determined by your lead objective and marketing strategy (biannual events for a maintenance strategy, quarterly events for a growth strategy). Your newsletter, when designed as a direct mail tool, should follow the same schedule. Let's say you plan to host quarterly events that you intend to promote via direct mail marketing and print media. This means you need to publish your newsletter every quarter. Conversely, if you intend to host biannual events, then you only need to publish your newsletter every six months.

After you work through the upcoming chapters on direct mail and print media, you'll have a complete understanding of how to integrate your newsletter's timing and content with all aspects of your promotional program. This information, in combination with the Event, Direct Mail, and Print Media Planners that are furnished in the *Marketing Plan Template*, will guide you in developing a synergistic promotional program.

Whatever publication frequency you select, avoid a monthly newsletter edition. It's logistically difficult and impractical to produce a high-caliber communication in this abbreviated time frame. Instead, devote your resources to turning out fewer, but higher-quality, issues.

The Collateral CD and DVD

A rather recent addition to the collateral materials family is the CD or DVD. Offered alone, or integrated into your community's Web site, these media enable you to expand upon your message and visual references through video and verbal presentations provided by a professional commentator, staff, or residents.

CDs and DVDs are a great sales tool when you're working with prospects who cannot easily visit your community. They are particularly indicated for communities that are preselling. With "virtual" technologies, you can offer a three-dimensional picture of the residence and lifestyle the prospect can expect once the community is complete.

The qualifier for the use of these media is whether you can afford them. CD and DVD production can be pricey endeavors, costing up to several thousand dollars per "finished minute." You'll need to weigh the costs against the contributions to sales to determine if a collateral CD or DVD is indicated for your program.

Controlling Costs

When correctly designed, your collateral materials can be one of the most expensive aspects of your marketing program, second only to staffing costs. However, there are a few ways to reduce costs.

A well-known tactic is to increase your print quantities with the investment of only a few more dollars. You should have a firm fix on the number of new leads the program intends to generate for the year (the lead objective), so you'll know how many brochures and inserts you'll need to provide to these eventual new inquirers. You also want to make sure you have enough stationery and introductory brochures to support your networking and direct mail campaigns. Save money by grouping "like jobs," such as your primary brochure and introductory brochure that share the same ink colors, and then go to press with these items at the same time. You can even print enough note cards to support your event promotions for the entire year. All you need to do is print a sufficient inventory of "blanks" at your first print run. Then, with each event you can customize the inside invitation through either LaserJet printing on the note card itself, or through a card inserted into the note jacket.

You can manipulate the design and the finish process to create further economies as well. If you have a logo that is highly stylized with four colors, foil, or embossing, it's a good idea to produce your stationery in two versions. The original is for external use and the second is a lower-cost adaptation for in-house use with staff and vendors.

> The penalty for piecemeal planning is that you pay a higher price for printing.

The central theme here is planning, planning, and more planning to avoid piecemeal printing and the penalty of higher pricing.

The most effective way to control costs and maximize your budget is to not waste it on off-target, inefficient, or counterproductive efforts that result from a "do-it-yourself" design route. Unfortunately, too many staff try to produce their own materials with in-house publishing software or work with a printer who does the layout (and printing) for them. While this method gives the appearance of being the least expensive, it is not without its challenges. If the staff is not experienced in both senior consumer marketing and the very technical aspects of design and printing, the cost of producing subpar materials far exceeds the cost of employing experienced marketing or agency support.

If you hire outside expertise, you need to be careful to select the right agency resource and to structure an advantageous and economical relationship. Ask for a written proposal and cost estimate, client references, and job samples to assess the firm's depth of experience. Make sure you understand what "deliverables" are included in the work scope. For example, who owns the artwork? You may not believe this, but technically the agency and the printer own the intellectual property, unless you specify otherwise.

Look for hidden costs and areas of potential cost overruns. For example, copywriting and creative design are very subjective processes and seldom will the involved parties come to agreement on submitted art and copy on the first go-round. Identify how many rounds of changes are included in the estimate and at what point in the revision process the agency begins to charge you for additional changes.

Specifically determine if the agency assesses a markup or commission for photography and printing. While this is a common billing practice, it's very expensive for you as the client and it also puts the agency's recommended course in a suspicious light. Is the agency recommending a particular paper stock or graphic approach because it will reap higher profit margins, or is the recommendation really what your program calls for? Be an aggressive negotiator and seek to eliminate this additional cost; insist on paying only for the agency's time and expertise.

Whether you choose to create collaterals yourself or to employ the support of an agency, remember this fundamental tenet: A consistent message conveyed through a cohesive design, and delivered to a carefully identified target market, is the best way to get Madison Avenue advertising results on a shoestring budget.

> While the right advertising can help you build and maintain a market presence, advertising alone will not increase your sales and occupancy.

11

Paid Media— Prerequisites To Advertising Success

Before we get into the sizzle of how to put together a high-profile direct mail, print media, and electronic media advertising campaign, we have to cover the conditions that must be present before any kind of paid media are employed in your marketing program.

While the right advertising program can help you build and maintain market presence, advertising alone will not increase your sales and occupancy. This point is so important—and so often misunderstood—that it needs to be said again: Advertising alone will not fill your building.

Advertising does nothing more than remove the "barrier of ignorance" about the presence of your community. It may increase lead activity, but as you know, leads are not sales. Too often, organizations will launch expensive advertising campaigns before they have implemented the preceding critical marketing components. As a result, leads are generated, but opportunities for sales are missed.

The industry's misuse of paid media brings to mind an old military axiom: Amateurs discuss strategy; experts discuss logistics. In our case, amateurs discuss advertising strategies; experts discuss marketing logistics. Splashy advertising will not compensate for a disjointed or deficient frontline marketing effort.

Test Your Readiness

Before you pursue any kind of advertising strategy, take the following quiz to determine if your program is prepared to employ paid media. You should be able to answer "yes" to each question.

Prerequisites-To-Advertising-Success Quiz

_____ Have you identified your market service area?

_____ Do you have a lock on your target market profile and their location within your market service area?

_____ Have you determined the lead and sales objectives and identified your marketing strategy?

_____ Does your community communicate a message of quality through the actions, attitudes, and appearance of the staff, and the appearance of the physical plant?

_____ Do you have adequate manpower to fulfill the sales objective?

_____ Has the marketing and sales team been trained and tooled to achieve the sales objective?

_____ Are your MKIS and lead-management protocols in place?

_____ Have you articulated the lead and sales objectives and the staff's performance goals to the team?

_____ Is the sales team meeting or exceeding the program's goals and objectives (prospect contacts, sales, and optimum close rate)?

_____ Has a grass roots networking program been fully implemented?

_____ Is there a special events plan in place?

_____ Is your marketing impression first-rate—from the appearance of your information center to the professional look and messages in your collateral materials?

_____ Do you have sufficient resources to invest in a "professionally" produced advertising program?

_____ Is your budget sufficient to sustain your advertising campaign over the course of the marketing program?

If you haven't been paying attention up to this point, these questions may seem overwhelming. However, they're intended to demonstrate simple marketing logic. What's the point of spending money on a Yellow Pages directory ad if your community is still struggling to answer the phone promptly and professionally? Why launch a direct mail campaign or run a newspaper ad with the goal of generating new leads, when what you really need is a new and better way to manage the leads you already have? Why would you pursue an expensive advertising campaign if you're receiving more than enough leads to secure your sales objectives from higher-value, referral-sourced leads? You get the point.

The Case Against Paid Media

Some of you may be thinking you can't possibly wait until you have all of the preceding marketing components lined out before you launch an advertising campaign. You're feeling the pressure—you need more leads and sales, and you need them now.

Well, sit down and take a breath, because creating leads and sales is precisely what *Inside Advice on Marketing Senior Housing* has been about up to now. The order in which the critical components have been presented is the order of their influence on lead generation and sales.

> By maximizing your use of lower-cost marketing components, you minimize your need for paid advertising.

Exceptional customer service, ample manpower, rigorous networking, and creative special events will produce the majority of your leads and sales. By maximizing your use of these fundamental, lower-cost marketing components, you minimize your need for, and dependence on, higher-cost advertising.

So if you need sales now, your marketing plan should begin with, and be deliberately weighted toward, the marketing components that have been presented thus far. The majority of your resources should be devoted to these components before you consider paid media.

This marketing premise may be too conservative for those who don't understand the elemental flow of integrated marketing and instead prefer to kick off their marketing effort with flashy advertising. Yes, some people use paid media, and they use it a lot. We all know that any advertising program will eventually produce some results if you throw enough money at it. But marketing success is not just about achieving your sales objective and occupancy goal. Marketing success is about hitting your goals with the best use of your resources. That's smart marketing.

For most of us, ambitious advertising is not an option because it is out of our economic reach, and that causes anxiety for those of you operating in a highly competitive market. Mailboxes are overrun with direct mail brochures; newspapers, radio, and television are filled with ads. You may be seeing more from your competitors than you'd like. However, just because the competition's advertising is visible doesn't mean its advertising is working. In fact, many communities use paid media, and especially newspaper, radio, and television advertising, for all the wrong reasons. These advertising media often are:

- Used by marketing directors because they are fast and easy to implement, especially in relation to the hard work of building consumer relations through expert sales practices, strong networking, and event marketing.
- Recommended by marketing or agency consulting firms for the very same reasons, and because the agency reaps attractive commissions.
- Pushed by overly aggressive media representatives who pressure marketing staff to make purchases by citing the competition's use of their medium. The media have identified a new target market—you. Most major media now feature senior-targeted publications and programs, all of which promise to be the sole and exclusive source for the mature market.
- Employed in response to the pressure to obtain exposure in a cluttered and crowded market. This pressure is often internal; it's common for a resident, management staff, or even a board member to ask, "Why aren't we in the newspaper this week—our competition is?"
- Used out of sheer vanity. There is nothing like the adrenalin rush of having your creative work showcased in a big glossy magazine ad or seeing your new community unveiled in a grand advertising campaign.

The Price-to-Value Relationship

Independent of your professional and personal opinion on the relative value of paid media, there is one aspect of media use that is abundantly clear to all seasoned marketers: Direct mail, newspaper, radio, and television advertising require consistent use in order to realize any measurable return. For example, it's fruitless to perform just one direct mail campaign, as is placing just one ad in the newspaper every several months. Your message will simply be lost in the media-saturated market. These media require long-term use to see a return. In other words, the effectiveness of direct mail, newspaper, radio, and television advertising is in direct proportion to the amount of recurrent exposure you generate, and the amount of money you spend.

Here's something else to consider. Direct mail, newspaper, radio, and television advertising are the most visible manifestations of a community's image. With these advertising media, you're communicating with thousands of individuals. As we learned in Chapters 9 and 10, you must have a top-notch, on-target image and message. So who's going to produce these high-impact advertising materials? Are you going to let the newspaper's 20-something-year-old graphics person paste something together for you? Or are you and your staff going to cobble together an ad?

> The effectiveness of paid advertising is in direct proportion to the amount of money you spend.

The point is this: You must work with experienced and industry-specialized creative and copywriting experts, at least initially, to turn out the best image. This resource is not an option when it comes to the use of high-profile media.

If you passed the Prerequisites-to-Advertising-Success Quiz, you're ready to explore the use of direct mail, print media, and electronic media in your marketing program. The following chapters provide an in-depth discussion on each medium's role and use, and the synergistic relationship that exists when these media are used in tandem.

If you found that you were lacking in the foundational program elements, then you will be spinning your wheels if you move ahead. Go back and do your groundwork.

> Direct mail is the high-powered rifle of every advertising arsenal. It enables you to precisely target those select few who qualify for your community, and do so on a one-to-one basis.

12

Direct Mail—The Right Tool For The Target Market

This chapter explores why direct mail is a favorite among professional marketers and the right tool to reach your target market. You'll learn how to hone in on your market with the best direct mail list, design materials that draw interest, and integrate direct mail with your print and electronic media campaigns to boost the overall performance of your paid advertising program.

Direct mail is the high-powered rifle of every advertising arsenal because it's particularly suited to the multi-faceted communication requirements of the senior housing industry. Given the very specialized nature of your product and services, and the unique profile of your target market, it makes little sense for you to gear your promotional efforts toward the general public using just newspaper, radio, or television advertising. First, it is unlikely that you can afford to employ these media on a consistent and sustained basis. Even if the resources were available, why would you spend money communicating with the market en masse when your message and services apply to only a few? So here's the beauty of direct mail: It enables you to precisely target those individuals who qualify for your community, and enables you to do so on a one-to-one basis. What could be better?

Another benefit of direct mail is that it gives you room to effectively communicate your message. Think about the businesses you're in. At minimum, you provide housing, services, and perhaps healthcare. Each of these areas has benefits that must be clarified in order for the consumer to understand your concept. It's tough to convey your offerings in a quarter-page newspaper ad or a 30-second radio spot. Direct mail, however, lets you tell your story, either in one well-designed communication or in a series of exposures over time.

Senior adults tend to prefer direct mail as well, or any printed medium, such as brochures, letters, newsletters, or postcards. Actually holding something in their hands allows them to absorb information at their own pace and appeals to their propensity to consume news and information through reading versus watching television or listening to the radio.

> Senior adults tend to prefer direct mail. It allows them to absorb information at their own pace.

It is also a concept-appropriate medium. There's something not quite right about seeing a newspaper ad for a major life change sandwiched in between ads for used-cars, laundry detergent, and lingerie—that is if it's even noticed. Think about how many times you've had to search for the location of your community ad in the newspaper!

Some marketers rebut the use of direct mail with the notion that your materials are lost in a sea of junk mail. That may be true for the general consumer, but not the senior consumer. We all know that for most older adults, meal times and mail times are the highlights of their days. This profile may change as the next generation enters our continuum in large numbers, but for now, we are still working with and serving a generation of readers.

Direct Mail Campaign Planning

The multiple benefits of direct mail don't mean that it's the only advertising tool that you use, or that it's used at the exclusion of other media. It only means that if you're working with limited resources, and most of us are, you'll get more mileage out of your advertising dollar when direct mail is the dominant medium in your advertising plan. You should plan your direct mail campaign for a 12-month period and it should correspond to your events and print media calendar. Your plan needs to identify with whom you will communicate (reach), what the message will be (piece), and how often you will communicate (frequency). You'll find the Direct Mail Planner in the *Marketing Plan Template* to be a helpful tool to outline these and other important program elements that we'll discuss in a moment.

Reach Out to the Market

Direct mail "reach" is agency lingo that refers to the number and type of individuals you intend to reach with your campaign. You have multiple potential audiences whose classifications should be familiar by now: wait-list, prospects, networking referral sources, and the general market (those age- and income-qualified households who have yet to inquire).

If you're in a maintenance marketing mode, you would direct your campaign to your primary audiences of wait-list, prospects, and select referral sources. In this scenario, direct mail is used to sustain and build interest. New leads would not be garnered, since you're mailing materials to individuals who have already inquired (or are already in your MKIS database). However, if you are in a growth marketing mode, where you need to increase leads, you would direct mail to these same audiences and also expand the scope of recipients to those households in your market area who have not inquired. This added reach is accomplished using a rented mail list.

The names and addresses of individuals in your market area can be obtained from companies that compile and publish this information. There are numerous vendors from which to choose. A quick Internet search using key words that contain "mail list senior market" will get you started. List vendors tout themselves as the ultimate direct mail database, with the ability to slice and dice your market by dozens of variables. In addition to the basic categories of age and income, these lists can be sorted by renters versus homeowners, gender, marital status, and all kinds of additional classifications from households-with-children to those with grandparents, mortgages, pets, and Internet connections.

While the more reputable sources guarantee that 95 percent of your materials will be delivered, their lists are only as strong as their data sources. Most rely on public records, such as phone books, to obtain their data. Look for vendors who disclose how their lists are compiled and how often they are updated. It's embarrassing to have a surviving spouse call you to take her deceased husband's name off your mail list.

> Keep your list parameters simple by using your market area and target market profile as the selection criteria.

Keep your list parameters simple by using your market area and target market profile as the selection criteria. Example criteria would be all households occupied by individuals age 65 and older, with incomes of $35,000 or more, who reside in your market area. Don't get too caught up with whether the suggested age is too young or the income too low. Remember: The higher the threshold that you set for age and income, the more households you eliminate. It's better to err on the side of sending too many mailers than sending too few. Besides, your mailing may end up in the hands of a daughter, who then shares it with a parent.

The Material Difference

At this level of marketing, you're well beyond sending a one-page flyer that has been copied on colored paper, and whose mail labels have been applied by you or your community's volunteers. Direct mail materials include personalized letters, introductory brochures, newsletters, and event- and theme-based invitations and postcards.

Introductory letters and brochures are used by new communities that are pre-marketing and mature communities that are introducing new units or a new program. As you learned in Chapter 10, the marketing newsletter is a mainstay that has multiple applications. Theme- and event-related postcards are a fast, fluid, and cost-effective tool to respond to emerging prospect profiles. As prospect profiles are captured through the MKIS, you can customize advertising themes to elaborate on selling points or to overcome product barriers. The event or theme that you promote in your invitation or postcard is also repeated in your newsletter and corresponding print ads.

Timing is Everything

Direct mail frequency should theoretically be determined by your lead objective and marketing strategy. If you have sufficient leads on hand to fulfill your sales objective (maintenance strategy), there is minimal need for direct mail. A biannual (twice a year) mailing (in combination with event marketing) is sufficient to sustain wait-list and prospect interest.

A growth marketing strategy requires a more intense direct mail schedule and extensive reach. In this situation, your frequency is essentially dictated by the time it takes to plan and execute a campaign. A comprehensive mailing from design to home delivery takes about 60 days. Therefore, the maximum number of sequential mailings you can conduct in a year would be six, with the ideal frequency being quarterly.

Of course, you could try to direct mail every month. However, what's the point of exposing your market to multiple disparate messages? Plan your program, interlock with events and print, and you'll have all the marketing synergy you need using a less ambitious schedule, and for less cost and effort.

The Direct Mail Marketing Matrix

You can simplify your direct mail planning and execution by following the Direct Mail Marketing Matrix (Figure 4). The Matrix correlates your direct mail target markets, materials, and frequency to your assigned marketing strategy. Use it in conjunction with the *Template's* Direct Mail Planner to work up your plan.

The Matrix indicates a biannual and quarterly schedule. These time frames also represent "advertising flights"—when your advertising occurs for an

FIGURE 4 Direct Mail Marketing Matrix

Strategy Frequency	Maintenance Biannually	Growth Quarterly
Target Markets	■ Wait-list ■ Lead base ■ Networking referral sources[1]	■ Wait-list ■ Lead base ■ Networking referral sources[1] ■ Qualified market
Materials Used	■ Newsletters ■ Event invitations or themed postcards	■ Personalized letters ■ Introductory brochure ■ Newsletters ■ Event invitations ■ Themed postcards

(1) Include (as appropriate) the additional target markets identified in your Strategic Networking Planner, such as residents, family members, staff, board members, volunteers/auxiliary, and community-based referral sources.

abbreviated, yet intense period. This technique allows you to maximize the impact of your advertising campaign during strategic times, particularly when direct mail is employed in conjunction with other paid media. For example, for a biannual direct mail frequency, your advertising flight would occur twice a year, April through May, and then again in September through October. During these two flight periods, your identified audiences would receive your newsletter, a theme-related postcard, or an invitation to an event that is hosted at the latter part of each period.

The Rate of Return

Now for the million-dollar question: What kind of response rate can you expect on your direct mail investment? A new community using direct mail for the first time will experience a response rate as high as 15 percent. The response rate drops to 1 to 3 percent for established communities that have flighted their market multiple times. These general response rates are presented with countless qualifiers and disclaimers. Each market responds differently to various forms of advertising, and your market may be the exception to the norm.

The first consideration is to base your response expectations on who is being targeted. If a rented list is employed, you should anticipate new leads.

Measure the response to each mailing through your MKIS. After you have sent two or three mailings to your market area zip codes, the high-producing zip codes should be isolated for continued cultivation. If you experience an inadequate response, as in few-to-no leads, you'll need to determine why. Was it the list, the theme, the materials, or the timing and frequency? Modify and continue your mailings to determine the formula that produces results.

> If your mailing is going to your wait-list or lead base, the phone is not going to ring off the hook.

If your mailing is only going to your wait-list or lead base, the phone is not going to ring off the hook. Your prospects already know about your community and the mailing acts as a supplement to your sales efforts. You're ensuring that when a prospect is ready to make the move, your community is foremost on their mind.

If the mailing is to promote event attendance, you should strive for and expect a response rate equal to your desired attendance goal. Be sure to promote the event in a provocative way to generate interest and provide clear instructions on what you want the reader to do—call or reply in writing with an RSVP.

Remember what we said earlier about education-themed event attendance: smaller is better. Expect, and be satisfied with, 25–30 responses. However, the overall return rate may be higher, especially if you're using in-tandem newspaper advertising and the ad is soliciting attendance as well as general inquiries of interest. If you're not generating the returns you need, then get on the phone and call your prospects. They'll have received your invitation, so it's not as if you're making a cold call. A personal phone call to solicit attendance is a good reason to contact your prospects, which is something you should be doing anyway.

Maximize Your Mailings

The mailer's design plays a key role in the response rate. It must be interesting, of high-impact, and motivate the recipient to respond, or at least hang onto your piece instead of tossing it into the trash. A good graphics firm or ad agency can acquaint you with some clever design techniques that will get your materials noticed, from provocative copy and colors to the use of "three-dimensional mailings," such as sending a gardening glove with an invitation attached to promote attendance to your upcoming gardening seminar.

Postal and letter-shop logistics affect the response rate, as well as how quickly the mailer arrives and whether it is returned as "undeliverable." The U.S. Post Office operates with lots of rules and requirements for obtaining bulk rate permits, business reply permits, bar codes, and postal indicia. If you're working with an experienced agency, you don't need to become a list and postal regulations expert. Your agency should be able to handle the entire process for you, from designing and printing your materials to home delivery.

If you're working solo, here are a few pointers to help you get the most out of your mailings:

- Avail yourself of the information and free guidance offered by mail list and letter-shop companies on how to meet the Post Office's postal and direct mail requirements. A "letter-shop" company is a firm that handles the tasks of storing, sorting, and applying labels to your direct mail materials and preparing your materials for acceptance and mailing by the U.S. Post Office. They can also locate and order a mail list for you.

- Always use first class postage for time-sensitive materials, such as an event mailing that has an RSVP date. Use lower-cost bulk-rate postage when time allows. Go with a bulk-rate stamp instead of an indicia to give your materials a more personal look.

- Any material sent as a personal invitation should be hand-addressed or LaserJet printed; never use mail labels.

- Be sure to add "Address Correction Requested" to your materials to clean up your list and avoid waste in future mailings.

- Whenever a reply coupon is used, make it easy for the recipient to return—it should be pre-addressed and postage paid. If a reply coupon is furnished as part of a letter mailing, include a pre-addressed, stamped envelope.

- Never send generic form letters—all correspondence should be customized to the name of the recipient.

- Don't use form letters to cull your prospect base. Many communities make the mistake of sending form letters to their prospects asking if they are still interested or if they want to remain on the mail list. If the sales team is interacting with its prospects, this kind of unintelligent and impersonal correspondence isn't necessary.

- The time of year has a huge impact on lead generation and is geography specific. Generally, the best direct mail flight times are January to April, May to June, and September to October.

- Avoid rented-list direct mail flight times that occur around the holidays, when your potential customer is blitzed with ads and holiday merriment. If individuals have not inquired before October, they probably are not going to during the holidays, unless there is a crisis.

- The winter months are a deadly time of year for snowbelt communities to tout a new lifestyle. The market has physically and mentally hunkered down for a long winter's nap or flown south for the season. Conversely, sunbelt communities may find winter to be an optimum time to target snowbirds.

These seasonal stipulations do not apply to your wait-list or lead base. Here you have a relationship established and it would be appropriate, and even timely, to interact with these groups around the holidays and during the dog days of summer or doldrums of winter. Your prospects' increased utility bills, yard labor, or snow-removal expenses make for great "solutions" theme-related mailings and may be just the trigger that moves them from idle interest to enthusiastic curiosity.

In the end, you have to use your own good instincts and your historical lead-analysis data about when to flight the market.

Electronic Mail

While "snail mail," or sending your materials through the U.S. Post Office, is the conventional form of direct marketing in our industry, a growing number of communities are using e-mail marketing in the same manner. Although it's an obvious communication tool when working with the adult child, the jury is out on whether this form of communication is preferred by senior adults over traditional direct mail. If you have the capabilities and resources, it makes sense to expand your direct marketing tactics to include this communication method, provided you have been diligent in obtaining prospects' e-mail addresses with associated permission to send information their way.

Whatever the direct mail medium used, its performance is boosted when blended with the right media mix. In the next chapter, we will discuss how to maximize your direct mail exposure and response rates through integrated marketing—pairing your direct mail materials with synergistic newspaper ads.

> You can't wing it when it comes to print media placement. When you advertise, and how much you advertise, must be carefully choreographed.

13
Print Media—How To Choose It And When To Use It

Media planning and buying has always been a technical area of advertising, or at least it can seem that way. The process has become even more complicated these days because print media outlets are working hard to compete with electronic media, particularly the Internet. To keep pace, newspapers, magazines, and directories are constantly changing their formats, sections, and content. Dozens of local, regional, and national publications have cropped up, all seeking to tap into the senior consumer market. Particularly if you're operating in a major metropolitan market, you have a head-spinning array of media options. Which ones should you use and how much should you spend? The answer to this advertising riddle is simple. Your print media placement and frequency is correlated to your marketing strategy.

You should use minimal to moderate advertising in a maintenance marketing strategy, where the objectives are to support your event and direct mail campaigns, and to keep a stock presence in a few publications or directories, such as the Yellow Pages. You're not dependent on, nor do you need, print media to generate leads.

In contrast, a growth marketing strategy requires aggressive advertising because there is a need to increase leads and/or maintain mind-share in a media-competitive environment.

Elements of a Print Media Campaign

Your print media campaign is really an extension of your networking, special events, and direct mail campaigns. If you have laid a good foundation in these components, your print media plan has started to take shape, in terms of what media you will use (categories), how often you will advertise (frequency), and what the message will be (themes).

There are several media categories from which to choose. Fortunately, these classifications can be linked to your marketing strategy, which in turn somewhat predefines your advertising frequency.

Major Dailies. Major dailies are the medium of choice when there's a need to substantially increase market awareness and leads. Although they are the most expensive medium, they also enjoy high readership due to their publication frequency.

Neighborhood Publications. Also referred to as "weekly" newspapers, these publications have fewer readers, but enjoy high readership within their locale. Typically, there is less ad clutter, and editorial content is based on local news and events. Neighborhood publications are generally a good value, with their low-cost (compared to major dailies) and respectable response rates. This medium is best suited to special event promotions and general maintenance marketing.

Specialty Publications. This category includes multiple miscellaneous media, ranging from tabletop quality magazines to local business and civic organization publications and programs. Business and civic group publications fall into the realm of goodwill advertising and their use is somewhat obligatory.

Directories. This category also contains a large and growing number of options, from the Yellow Pages and senior housing guides and publications, to Chamber of Commerce directories. The number of telephone directories alone in a typical market is enough to give you a headache. Senior housing directories are equally pervasive. A certain amount of targeted directory representation is mandatory. The key is to select the right ones and run the right ad size.

Billboard Advertising. Billboard advertising is the placement of your print ad on outdoor media, such as road signs or bus wraps. It's a very expensive mass marketing vehicle that is geared toward a high-speed and highly mobile consumer—not the senior adult consumer. This medium is mentioned in passing because some providers use it, not because it's recommended. It's a lousy advertising choice—so much so that it doesn't rate further discussion.

Ad Frequency and Flights

If you're pursuing a maintenance marketing strategy, you should be hosting biannual events that are being promoted to your wait-list and lead base through direct mail. You would advertise these events in your neighborhood publications at a frequency of one to two times for each event per publication. If your budget allows, you can also run an occasional "general awareness" ad in the regular or special edition section of a neighborhood publication.

For a growth marketing strategy, event frequency is increased to quarterly, as is your use of direct mail marketing and print media to promote the events. A growth marketing strategy also employs the use of general awareness advertising that is integrated with your direct mail schedule. For example, let's say you're sending out a brochure or an awareness postcard to your prospect base and a rented list. At the same time, you would run visually integrated ads in major dailies and neighborhood publications.

Use advertising flights to maximize your print media impact. For instance, during the months of March and April, you would run the same awareness ad at a frequency of four to six times per month. In May, you would run an ad that promotes the event you are hosting (in late May), at a frequency of four to six times. In June, you would not advertise at all. In July, you would recommence your print media campaign, using the same advertising frequency and ad rotation just described. This scheme is repeated over the course of your campaign.

The same advertising flight concept is employed even in a maintenance marketing strategy where your use of print media is minimal. Short-term saturation is always more effective than running an ad once a month over several months.

All campaigns should be anchored with credible editorial coverage. The only way this will happen is if you submit press releases that tie-in to your advertising theme and media placement schedule.

Integrated Themes—Line Out the Layout

When it comes to print ad design, be sure to apply the copywriting and design concepts presented in Chapter 9. Get rid of the bullet copy and visual clutter, don't oversell and crowd your ads, and make sure they visually integrate with your established graphic template. An event ad is especially easy to produce—it's a likeness of the layout used in your direct mail materials. Be very clear in your ads on what it is you want the reader to do: to call for more information (display a prominent phone number), mail in the coupon contained within the ad, or RSVP for a special event.

For general awareness ads, it's important to stay with a few well-selected themes rather than constantly changing your message. The idea is to build market recognition. A quarter-page ad is generally sufficient and is superior to a small credit-card-sized ad or a larger and more expensive half-page ad. If you plan ahead, you can make a general awareness ad pull double duty—turn it into an event ad just by adding a snipe to the headline area.

It's also a good idea to invest in a stock ad for use in local business and civic group publications and senior housing guides. Your community name, tag line, and contact information are all that are required for this kind of ad. Besides, these publications are not the place to educate the market. Set aside a limited amount of money for these publications and limit your exposure to what you have budgeted. You can spend yourself broke if you respond to every fraternal and civic organization that solicits advertising in its directory.

> Senior adults don't shop for a serious life change by consulting the phone book.

Telephone directories are an area where marketers grossly overspend. Be critical in your assessment of their value by examining the number of sales that are generated from any directory that you use. The Yellow Pages is often touted as a good lead source, which assumes that inquiring individuals use a telephone directory to learn about retirement living options. The truth is, these individuals probably knew about your community already, and they used the Yellow Pages to find your number. Let's get real: Senior adults don't shop for a serious life change by consulting a phone book. Forget about what the competition is doing and stay with a clean and simple in-column listing or credit-card-sized display ad in select directories.

When It's Okay to Advertise More

There are exceptions to these universal advertising parameters. If you're pre-marketing a new community, your print media program will be dramatically different—as in considerably more intense and more expensive. It would be dominated by awareness advertising (versus event advertising), and the frequency would be higher.

The same scenario holds true for a mature community that is expanding. Not only must you maintain occupancy in your current product, but you must also generate leads and sales for the new product. This is a tall order to fill. You'll need to augment all your marketing systems, from added manpower to aggressive direct mail and newspaper advertising. Any new development is a high-risk venture, so do whatever it takes to achieve the lead and pre-sales objectives.

Another exception to the rule is the highly competitive market, where providers are competing for more than market share; they are also competing for mind-share. Consumers in these glutted locales are bombarded from every media direction about the growing number of housing and healthcare alternatives. This environment presents a marketing predicament for a mature community. Although it may have a solid wait-list or lead base and enjoy strong lead activity, the competition's high-impact advertising can turn heads away from the established provider and toward new projects. This circumstance mandates that the mature community use print media just to preserve its market position. If your community fits this profile, be sure to discuss the media-intense environment in your marketing plan as justification for your increased use of newspaper advertising. You'll also need to determine whether the additional advertising results in increased lead activity. Your marketing success will need to be measured by your ability to sustain your preeminent market position and associated lead activity in the face of increasing competition, as opposed to occupancy gains.

Assessing the Response Rate

While we're on the subject of performance, you're probably wondering what type of response to expect from your print media advertising. It used to be you could anticipate a return of 10 new leads per exposure, assuming that it's a general awareness ad and not an event ad. However, industry average response rates are becoming an inferior baseline for measuring your program's performance, especially when it comes to print media. As with direct mail, it's almost impossible to cite an "average" response rate because so many variables, such as type of media used, timing, frequency, theme, and graphic execution influence the response rate. Moreover, the industry average is based on leads, not sales, which is a truer performance measure.

Also keep in mind that your entire promotional program is designed to accomplish synergistic marketing. The benefit is an increased response rate and cost savings. You'll know that all components are working together when you notice that the lines begin to blur on lead sources. People may know about your community because they live in the area. They receive your direct mail materials and they see your ads. They may even attend an event (that they also saw advertised in their neighborhood paper). So which of these sources first caused them to inquire? Who knows? Even if your team is queued up to profile lead source, and you've been zealous about tracking and analyzing lead source data, it is difficult to definitively gauge print media performance using a simple lead count when so many forces are at play.

> Use your MKIS to determine whether your print media is producing results.

The key is to use good judgment and your MKIS to determine early and assess often whether your print media plan, in combination with your event and direct mail marketing program, is producing results as measured in leads, and more importantly, sales. The aggregate data tells you what aspects of your advertising program are working and makes real clear what media are not working and need to be eliminated or modified.

The Print Media Plan

You can't wing it when it comes to print media selection and placement. When you advertise, and how much you advertise, must be carefully choreographed. The following chronological action steps outline what has to happen for you to develop your program. The *Marketing Plan Template* will guide you in assimilating your plan and there is a Print Media Planner for you to summarize your campaign.

Define your overall print media strategy. Are you using a minimal to moderate amount of print media as a supplement to your event and direct mail program or are you intensively using print media for the mass marketing tactics of increasing awareness and leads?

Research your media outlets. If you haven't already done so, contact all market area media and obtain a "media kit." This packet includes all the information you need to ascertain the medium's geographic coverage in relation to your market area, its geographic reach in relation to the zip codes being targeted in the direct mail campaign, and its general cost per ad or cost per column inch. Also make note of special sections or features geared toward the senior adult market.

Investigate price and payment options. Pay attention to the additional ways media encourage you to buy more space through multiple discount methods. Major daily advertising zones are available at a substantially lower cost than a "run of paper" (ROP) purchase. For those of you unfamiliar with this concept, know that big newspapers divide their publications into zones or geographic sectors. You can limit your advertisements to run in selected zoned publications that should overlay with your market service area, as well as correspond to your direct mail flight pattern. You'll need to research publication media kits for a full explanation of this concept, available options, and corresponding costs.

Frequency, repeat, pick-up, standby, and non-profit rates are additional ways to reduce cost. Discounts vary by media and market, so a simple explanation isn't possible here. Just be aware that you can reduce your per-ad cost as much as 50 percent or more by thoroughly investigating your options. Media representatives are more than happy to work with you in media selection and buying. One caveat: Their job is to sell space and a lot of it, so always scrutinize their recommendations and contrast them to your objectives.

Identify your creative themes. Within your selected strategy, what are the themes you want to employ? Are you hosting a series of seminars? Are you announcing a new product or service? Are you attempting to generate interest in your community? Identifying your themes in advance makes it easier to determine where to place your ads.

Define the specifications. For each theme, you need to plan the associated number of ads that need to be produced. You can also outline the ad's specifications in terms of its size, visual and copy elements, and response mechanism.

Calculate print media frequency. Determine the number of ads you will run for each theme, and for each medium. Prepare a calendar that illustrates the frequency by date, by month, or by quarter.

Determine how you will produce and place your ads. In doing so, consider the design and production needs of your collateral material and direct mail program. When looking at your total program requirements, you may conclude that it's time to secure the support of an advertising agency, to at least provide start-up support. Once the graphic portfolio and creative templates are established, you can manage the program on your own.

Identify how you will track and analyze media performance. Always make sure your marketing information and lead-management software data fields are current. Track media used, themes, and dates. Your advertising tactics must be continuously analyzed over the term of the program to repeat successful program elements (media and themes) and eliminate obvious nonperforming media. Nonperformance is defined as low-to-no value in: 1) generating qualified leads and sales, and 2) complementing the performance of other promotional components, such as events and direct mail marketing.

Print media is effective if used wisely and for the right reasons. Just make sure you know why you are using it and plan your tactics accordingly.

> You should be able to achieve your lead and sales objective without the use of radio and television advertising if you have laid the right marketing foundation.

14

Electronic Media—Broadcast Basics To Reach The Masses

We've come a long way and covered a lot of marketing components since Chapter 1. You now know how to analyze your market, calculate your lead and sales needs, configure your sales and marketing manpower, plan events, and implement a direct mail and print media campaign. This chapter heads you toward the home stretch. It's about the final promotional component—electronic media—which includes radio and television, as well as the youngest communication entry, the Internet.

Let's discuss radio and television first, since these two media share similar attributes.

One phrase sums up the power of radio and television: mass-market advertising (hence the name "broadcast"). To get up to speed on these media, just contact your local radio or television sales representatives to give you the lowdown on your many options here. They'll be more than happy to acquaint you with the capabilities and "value" of broadcast advertising. You'll be provided with lots of facts and figures on audience profiles, listening or viewing times, and the CPM (cost per thousand) of taking your message into the homes of your target market. They'll even offer to cut a substantially discounted contract rate and have the station produce your radio or television ad for free! It's a tempting deal, but as a prudent marketer you have to stop and consider if broadcast is really a practical and suitable addition to your media mix. In most cases, the answer is no, it's not.

Suitable Strategies or Senseless Overload?

Practically speaking, most communities simply do not need to employ broadcast advertising if they have implemented the critical components that *Inside Advice on Marketing Senior Housing* has presented. We've already discussed the relative merits of a marketing effort designed to reach your target market as opposed to blanketing the masses who may not have any interest in your community. Your fundamental marketing components (customer service, sales, networking, and events), complemented by a thoughtful advertising strategy (integrated direct mail and print media), should be clicking off more than a sufficient number of leads and sales. If not, double back to determine what components need finetuning before you layer on yet another level of advertising.

A standard operating procedure for any marketing program is to round out your well-planned direct mail and print advertising program with the costless side of electronic media. Rather than buying broadcast time, use these media as a way to extend your networking endeavors. Just as you did with print advertising, electronic media outlets should be loaded in your database, made part of your focus market hit list, and furnished with press releases on newsworthy items and community event calendars.

It takes a cool head and steely determination to limit your use of broadcast to good press relations. If you're working in a media-intense, competitive market, nothing will make your palms sweat like having your primary competitor roll out a jazzy radio or glitzy television commercial. If you're following the marketing mantra presented in Chapter 1, "Chase the customer, not the competition," you're not going to let the other guy's activities sway your solid marketing strategy. You're smart enough to know there may be other factors causing your competition to advertise more than you do. Perhaps a heavy-handed administrator or board member insisted on running some radio commercials in a desperate attempt to buoy a sinking ship or massage an inflated ego. Maybe the marketing director bought into the same sales pitch that you got from the same media outlet. Or maybe the staff hasn't noticed that the incoming leads being generated by these media are not income-qualified.

> It takes a cool and steely determination to limit your use of broadcast to good public relations.

When it comes to the use of radio and television advertising, you really have to step back and consider whether broadcast is a good fit with the senior adult market. At first glance, broadcast is kind of sexy. There's your name splashed on the television screen or resounding over the radio airwaves. If you rely solely on published guides (Arbitron or Nielsen) that track who is watching television and listening to the radio at any given time, you'll find our market tends to be a devoted group; they even comprise the majority of the audience for certain shows.

But here's the catch: Radio and television are fast-paced media. The listener has to acquire information at the pace set by the broadcaster—usually a 30-second spot. That presents a twofold challenge. First, you have to sum up, in quick order, the complex benefits of your community. This is one area where electronic media come up short, as compared to say, direct mail, that gives you enough room to tell your multi-faceted story. Second, because of age-associated sensory changes, this rapid-fire, forced-pace format is a less than ideal medium for communicating with senior adults. Background noise, the tone of the announcer's voice, rate of speech, and even the amount of time a phone number is repeated or left on the screen affect comprehension. So while your message may be seen or heard, is it being understood?

If you decide to use radio or television beyond the requisite public service announcements, you're now working without a net. Unlike direct mail and print, you won't find any handy little industry templates, grids, or formulas for when and how often to use broadcast. You have only your common sense to guide you, and the assistance (and cost) of an ad agency or your local media outlets, who operate with enlightened self-interest, to show you how their stations will put you in the spotlight.

You Still Need a Plan

If you're rolling out these mass-marketing cannons, you'll need a media plan, similar in detail to that of your print media plan. The broadcast terrain is larger than print, and more complicated. Do you want national or local exposure? What programming options deliver the best return—broad-based shows like the news, or specific programming developed around personalities or subjects? For television, you'll also need to identify your options for network and cable advertising.

A broadcast media plan may seem like overkill if you're only interested in running a commercial on a local cable channel that is offering a spot for a price you just can't pass up. In that case, just plow right ahead. This tactic doesn't make much sense to begin with, so what's the point of a plan?

If you can't be swayed and still want to be on the airwaves, here are some suggestions to keep you from being burned.

Don't skimp on frequency and duration. Most campaigns require a six-week saturation to realize returns and to measure true effectiveness.

Hire a production pro. This is no time for amateur, do-it-yourself advertising.

Be evocative and engaging, but avoid sensory confusion. Stay with a few simple concepts and repeat them often. Pace the content and speed of the message delivery, avoid background noise, and use a pleasant, well-modulated voice. For television commercials, use clear graphics and images that show viewers your benefits, instead of just telling them. Always make sure the images are in accord with what is being said. Respect the creative and copy signature established in your collaterals, direct mail, and print campaigns.

Be aware that the majority of radio programming is geared to a younger, more mobile market that caters to drive-time listeners. That's the downside if you're interested only in the senior adult market. However, if your community offers assisted living or long-term care, radio is a respectable tool for reaching the adult child who tunes into his or her favorite station during drive times.

Try to determine your place in the commercial queue. Be aware of the "tune out" factor, where listeners change channels soon after commercials begin to run. Try to control where you are in the commercial lineup so your spot can be heard before listeners tune out.

Be clear on why you are using broadcast and how you will measure your results. Broadcast advertising is one area of advertising where there is a lot of smoke but little fire. The phone will ring, but it may not be an age- and income-qualified prospect on the line. If your goal is to generate broad market awareness, state this in your media plan, and understand that an expense is being incurred for which there is no direct, tangible return. However, if broadcast is being used with the expressed goal of generating leads, then you'll need to assess its value in generating leads and sales in relation to its cost, and in relation to the performance of direct mail and print. This finite tracking is a challenge if your campaign is using all three media simultaneously.

Getting Wired for the Web

While this advertising tool is last in our electronic lineup, it's only because of its relatively recent debut. The Internet really belongs at the head of the class because it's fast becoming a marketing mainstay.

For a generation that is supposed to be averse to automated communications and doing business with machines (instead of people), the mature market has surprised us with its growing use of the World Wide Web. More and more older adults are being coaxed online by their families, who find that a desktop computer, complete with Internet access, makes the perfect Christmas gift. Plus, in today's mobile society with scattered families, the Internet is a fast and economical way to share experiences. Its use will only expand with every generation.

Designing Your Site

Your community must have a Web site. However, that doesn't mean the marketing department is responsible for developing and maintaining the site. Web-based technology is moving at warp speed and the present and future scope and applications of an organization's Web site far exceed marketing's purview.

For example, what audiences does the organization intend to serve with its Web site? Should there be an Intranet or Weblog to enable communication with residents, staff, or other stakeholders? Does the organization envision a time when resident application intake can be accomplished electronically through its Web site? If your community offers health and wellness programming and home care, does the organization foresee a future when these services will be augmented by telemedicine? The possibilities are limitless.

> Your community must have a Web site. However, that doesn't mean the marketing department is responsible for its development.

Here are a few highlights on Web page design. The discussion is on the marketing-related aspects of the site and not all facets of Web site engineering.

Define the information scope. Leadership consensus must be reached on the scope of information to be covered on your Web pages—both the home page and the gateway pages. A gateway page is a sub-page of the home page that caters to a specific audience, either by providing information that addresses the needs of that audience, or by aggregating information by subject. Common topics include the organization's history and mission, a welcome and introduction, employment and volunteer opportunities, fund development and solicitation, and general news and events. Mind you, this is a list of common subject matter, not recommended subject matter.

Ensure an integrated design. While it is not for marketing to determine the Web site's information scope, you'll want to police its design. The pages should employ a graphic and copy approach similar to your other marketing communication materials. You have to assume that the primary visitor is an older adult, and therefore the design must be easy to follow, easy to navigate, and not overly busy. Small type sizes, garish colors, and gratuitous or flashy design elements will drive your traffic down, not up. Revisit the rules of good advertising design and copy presented in Chapters 9 and 10. Your Web site design is no different.

Pace information. When it comes to featuring marketing and sales information on your Web site, think of these pages as an electronic version of select collateral materials—specifically your primary brochure. However, do not publish your floor plan or pricing information. Hold this information back for use during fulfillment. Remember, the goal is the same as when prospects call your community for the first time—to get them in for a personal visit. If customers can obtain all the information they seek via your Web site—why should they bother talking to you? Or, if they obtain most of your key material via your site, and then request and receive the same by mail, where's the value? This concept applies to senior adults, not the adult child market—they want it all, and they want it now. Your target market profile ultimately dictates what information, and how much information, to furnish on your Web site.

Be an information resource. As you have done with all paid advertising components, represent your community as a purveyor of news and resources of value to older adults. Offer a learning library or a news center on articles of interest to the target market. Promote attendance to upcoming events (as long as you provide a response mechanism). Feature relevant articles that appear in your newsletter. If you're reaching out to caregivers, be sure to include resource materials for their benefit as well, so they can facilitate a parent's care or decision-making process. Many communities even feature their collateral CD/DVD (as discussed in Chapter 10) as part of their Web site or as part of their fulfillment package.

You also need to determine how you'll direct the market to your Web site. Of course, one method is to feature your Web site address in all your collateral materials, direct mail, and print media ads. However, what about the rest of the world that has not been exposed to your marketing communication materials? You'll need to work with a Webmaster to make sure that your community is linked to multiple search engines such as Google, America Online, and Yahoo, and that your listing comes out at the top of page one instead of page ten of the search results. A Webmaster can also keep the organization's Web pages current.

Clearly, in terms of electronic media, the Internet is the place to put your attention and resources. As we learned in the previous chapter, the lure of flashy ads can be strong. Choose your advertising tools wisely, keeping in mind who your audience is and how it can best receive your message.

> Marketing roles have been expanded and results are demanded. Scanty outlines and Post-it Notes won't cut it anymore. You need a plan to guide your efforts.

15

Marketing Plan, Time Line, And Budget— Drafting The Document

You may be wondering why the administrative aspect of marketing—the marketing plan, time line, and budget—is the last critical component that we cover, instead of the first. The reason is simple: Before you learn how to write and cost out a marketing plan, you must first understand the components that make up a marketing plan. Now that you have a solid understanding of the critical components of marketing, it's time to document, in the form of a marketing plan, where you are now, where you intend to go, and how you will get there.

Most of us have a natural tendency to avoid the documentation process. The notion of hammering out a comprehensive plan may seem like a daunting assignment. It's just one more item to add to your never-ending task list. Or, you may be a shoot-from-the-hip type who prefers to bypass the bureaucratic paperwork and just get the job done. Old-school marketers seem to have the hardest time documenting their destination. They know how to "get there" without a marketing tome that tells them what they need to do.

Alas, times have changed, not just within the industry, but also in the expectations an organization has of its marketing function. Competition has catapulted the subject of marketing to the top of an organization's list of strategic initiatives and the heat is on. Marketing roles have been expanded, expectations have been raised, accountability is expected, and results are demanded. Scanty outlines and Post-it Notes just won't cut it anymore. You need a plan to guide your efforts. The organization's stakeholders require a plan in order to understand your efforts.

The Politics of Planning

The time invested in drafting a document that explains what you intend to do pays dividends. Here's why:

A good marketer is a good manager—and a good manager always has a plan. Good managers endeavor to shape their operational environment within the organization. They educate their superiors and departmental peers on their department's role. They lobby to obtain the resources and support necessary to simultaneously fulfill their program objectives and support their departmental staff. Good marketing managers use a written marketing plan to educate key constituents on the marketing agenda and initiatives. They are adept at "selling" to their internal customer base (management), while they also sell to their external markets.

A proactive marketing plan, grounded in research, is the best way to ward off the steady stream of polite ideas and strong-arm suggestions on how to fill your building. There are two kinds of marketing programs: situation-driven and market-driven. Unfortunately, the most common is situation-driven, where everything but good information and intuition steers your marketing direction as you react to whatever comes down the pike. Instead of a cohesive marketing process, there is chaos. If you experience a period when sales are slow, you have everyone breathing down your neck asking why, wanting more sales, and providing lots of ideas on how to get them. Your superior returns from a conference all lathered up about a new marketing idea touted by a consultant and wants you to revamp your program, or worse, wants to hire the consultant to help you do your job. You just can't seem to move those few remaining one-bedroom apartments, so the best fix must lie in changing the unit mix. Situation-driven marketing lurches from one fix to another, without ever realizing any sustained improvements or momentum.

In contrast, a market-driven program—one in which you have carefully followed the critical components and produced a well-thought-out, information-based plan, sets the marketing course and keeps it on course.

A marketing plan dispels prima donna perceptions. An organization's success depends on marketing and operations working hand-in-hand, making equal contributions. Marketing's role is to direct consumers to the community (revenue), while operations' role is to meet the needs of the customers (expense). This textbook description, however, belies the tension that can accompany the relationship. It is not uncommon for the operations team to think that marketing "oversells" or that the marketing process is about a lot of expensive fluff. We're seen as those "people who sell."

The reference is understandable: Every day, operations sees marketing and sales staff stroll about the community chatting with customers, fluffing pillows, fussing over food service, pressing to get apartments painted, passing out pretty brochures, and presto, just like magic, we meet our occupancy goal. If only it were so easy.

> A formal marketing plan sets the record straight and illustrates that there is more to marketing than hosting a garden party.

A formal marketing plan, developed in conjunction with operations, sets the record straight and illustrates that there is more to marketing than hosting a garden party.

A plan empowers your organizational role, and helps secure resources. A major marketing grievance is insufficient funds to do a sufficient job. Comments like, "they won't let me," "it's too expensive," or, "it's not in the budget" are all too familiar refrains offered up by marketers as rationales for an inadequate effort. Staff sit at their desks, like helpless victims, mewing about their limited authority and small budgets.

Well, you won't find any sympathy for your situation here. The reason your operating purview and marketing budgets are limited is that, without a game plan, management has no idea what it's going to take to get the job done, how much money you need, and how it will be used.

The Marketing Plan Template

Suppose you're a business owner who intends to implement a marketing program that is going to cost $100,000. You don't have that much operating cash, so you approach your local bank for a loan. Do you think you could provide a bank officer with a verbal presentation and two-page action plan of your needs and receive $100,000? No. The bank is going to ask for a marketing plan that demonstrates the program's objectives and its corresponding costs and returns. Likewise, without a well-authored marketing plan, your organization is not going to provide you with carte blanche resources.

A marketing plan communicates the program's goals, objectives, strategy, tactics, time line, and budget. Rather than get bogged down in an esoteric discussion of the theories and principles of these plan elements, we have made the planning process less complicated. We've eliminated the filler and replaced it with the substance of what you need to know.

Goals, Objectives, Strategy, and Tactics

The dictionary defines a plan as a systematic arrangement of elements or important parts, a configuration or outline. *Inside Advice on Marketing Senior Housing* has already enumerated the critical elements of your marketing plan—they are the chapters of this book. The plan's goal is your occupancy objective. The objectives are your lead and sales targets. The strategy is maintenance or growth. The tactics are what has to happen to achieve the plan's objectives, organized as marketing components.

These components form a ready-made roadmap for you to follow. To make it even simpler, the *Marketing Plan Template* (on CD) condenses the book's information into a step-by-step guide, complete with action steps, worksheets, and planners to write your own plan.

However, you are not ready to go there just yet. There are two remaining plan elements that need to be covered: the time line and the budget. When we're done, you'll find that writing your plan is as easy as filling in the blanks.

Two Types of Time Lines

Your marketing plan needs to address two time lines: 1) the program's overall time frame, and 2) the time it will take to plan and implement the individual components, and to realize results in the form of leads and sales.

For most marketing plans, the overall time frame is a 12-month period. It usually correlates to the organization's fiscal or calendar budgetary period. If your plan calls for a pre-marketing launch of new units, the plan's time frame is longer, around 18 to 24 months, to marry with the development timetable and the pre-sales objectives.

The time required to plan and implement each component, and the time required to bring in leads and sales, plays an even larger role in forecasting the program's "real-time" schedule versus the basic 12-month budgetary planning cycle.

For example, consider the marketing and sales manpower component. Depending on your objectives, you may need to advertise for, interview, and select additional staff, or reconfigure the duties and responsibilities of your current staff. Staff must then be trained in sales and lead-management protocols, which by the way, also have to be enhanced or developed. This one marketing component alone can take three months or more to put in place (Figure 5).

Envisioning and executing the plan's promotional components are especially laborious and protracted. Special events, for example, must be planned for and advertised months in advance. Writing, designing, and printing collateral materials can take up to three months. Direct mail design and production can take the same amount of time, in addition to the time required for mail list procurement, printing, and mailing.

Chapter 15 Marketing Plan, Time Line, and Budget–Drafting the Document

Unfortunately, a lot of management and marketing staff fail to take the start-up time into account. Occupancy gains are often incorrectly projected to begin in the first or second month of the budget period, without regard to the time it will take to make these gains happen. When the sales or occupancy targets are not achieved as planned, everyone panics; staff assume that the marketing program is not working and scramble to implement knee-jerk tactics to make up for perceived lost ground. In reality, all that was wrong was a naïve notion about marketing turnaround times and a too-ambitious time line for occupancy gains.

There are no shortcuts to the groundwork of putting a program into place, so be realistic on component turnaround times and align your sales and occupancy expectations accordingly. The larger the to-do list, the longer it will take to make it happen.

> There are no shortcuts to putting a program into place. The longer the to-do list, the longer it will take to make it happen.

If you're a new community mobilizing a marketing effort for the first time, or an occupancy-challenged community that is formalizing or correcting its marketing practices, you can anticipate it taking no less than three months, and most likely six months, to realize occupancy gains.

This is particularly the case for communities with chronic vacancies. It took months, and perhaps even years, for occupancy problems to brew and boil over, and it may take an equal amount of time to dig out and reverse the decline.

These time frames are also necessary for marketing due diligence. Until you have all program components in place, fully integrated and monitored, you do not have the information necessary to determine the reasons for your success or failure.

FIGURE 5 Manpower Gantt Chart

Month/Task	1	2	3	4	5	6	7	8	9	10	11	12
Assess staff roles	■											
Realign staff duties		■										
Define performance goals		■										
Recruit new sales person			■									
Select training consultant			■									
Train staff				■				■				■
Assess performance				■	■		■		■		■	

The best way to assimilate your time lines is to assign a beginning and end date to each marketing component. You don't need fancy project management software; just use the *Template's* Gantt chart or calendar sheets. This visual representation of a 12-month marketing period is also a good way to depict planned versus actual performance. The Gantt in Figure 5 illustrates a time line for augmenting marketing manpower (with the goal of producing more sales). While work on this area began at the first of the year, a return, in the form of sales, will not be realized until the fifth month (post-training).

You can also create economies of scale and achieve cost savings when you know your program requirements for the entire year. For example, you can forecast annual quantities and take advantage of volume discounts for collateral material printing, mail list rental, and newspaper advertising. Graphic themes can be developed with an eye toward future needs so your advertising materials can be designed for double duty. One well-conceived theme ad can be easily converted into a direct mail postcard, newsletter insert, or special event ad with the use of a snipe.

How specific you are in listing tasks in your Gantt chart or calendar depends on how much detail you need to make sure the written plan is translated into timely action. For example, if you're scheduling a direct mail campaign, you can note just the start and stop times for the total campaign or detail each task, from copywriting to home delivery.

> Detailed tasks and time lines go a long way toward illustrating the intense work that precedes seemingly simple results.

You may be inclined to shortcut this task-time documentation, since you know what needs to happen and when. However, before you do, stop and think about who else within the organization will be reading and approving the plan, and decide if more detail would be helpful in communicating the depth and breadth of the program. For example, management may be unaware of the time and effort involved in hosting an event or executing a comprehensive advertising campaign. Detailed tasks and time lines go a long way toward illustrating the intense work that precedes seemingly simple results.

Marketing planning and implementation may seem like a marathon. However, keep in mind that once the initial investment of time is made to get a new component up and running, or an existing component augmented and operational, you can drop back to repeating various tasks and abbreviate your documentation.

For instance, after your customer service, lead-management, and strategic networking practices have been established, the tasks and time lines simply need to reflect the ongoing activities that will be performed throughout the year. It will take many months to develop or enhance a complete collateral package, but once established, it's a matter of inventory control and supplying the materials necessary to support your direct mail campaign.

Budgetary Assumptions

Many organizations enter the budgetory planning process with the wrong attitude and assumptions. This mind-set results in insufficient funding and inadequate results. If an organization tries to meet its budgetary goals by balancing its books with marketing cutbacks or miserly spending, the organization will not meet its revenue goals. Any macroeconomics course will teach you that administrative amateurs meet their budgetary goals by cutting and controlling expenses. Business executives meet and exceed their budgetary goals by growing the revenue side of the business (occupancy) and controlling expenses. In its purest form, marketing generates revenue. Why hamper revenue growth with penny-pinching constraints?

> If an organization tries to meet its budgetary goals by balancing its books with miserly marketing funding, it will not meet its revenue goals.

Every organization, especially those seeking to improve occupancy, wants to compress the marketing process and maximize occupancy and revenue. Unfortunately, this isn't going to happen unless you're willing to invest in the added resources necessary to ramp up your program. You can't advance your marketing effort without advancing your resources. The speed of marketing execution is directly dependent on the resources, in the form of people, devoted to the process. You'll see faster results if you staff your program with more sales representatives, arm yourself with a professional advertising agency, and let an experienced marketing consultant or expert marketing director establish and control your program. Do not expect a staff of one or two to single-handedly plan and execute a mighty marketing effort—and by the way, also sell units—all on a reed-thin budget. This approach only results in anemic sales and occupancy gains that occur at a painfully slow pace.

These observations, however, should not be interpreted as a cavalier disregard for financial accountability and control, or a ticket to frivolous or excessive spending. The presented marketing components are designed to achieve the highest and best use of resources, optimum economies of scale, and a quantified return. At this level of marketing, information systems are also in place to continuously monitor program performance (and its expense in relation to return) and allow immediate course and cost correction.

There is only one way to create a marketing budget and that is to market by component, and not by budget. Identify your program's components and corresponding tasks, and then identify the costs associated with the implementation of these tasks. Starting with a fixed budget sum and then forcing your marketing program into this fixed amount will not produce results because the plan is being contorted to fit some arbitrarily assigned sum of money. The same applies to the use of nebulous "cost-per-unit" or "cost-per-sale" formulas to forecast your budget. They have absolutely no relevance to your community.

We can't tell you what your budget should be, but we can suggest how your budget should be constructed and monitored. First, if you don't know the general principles of accounting, or how your organization's financing and accounting function works, now is a good time to learn the basics. Management is more than willing to show you how to improve financial accountability.

At this stage of the game, financial accountability means you can't get away with grouping your expenses into generic accounting categories such as "salaries," "promotions," or "advertising." That may be how you presently classify your expenses, which may be an offshoot of how your organization accounts for marketing costs, but this method doesn't cut it for your budgetary planning needs. Each marketing component should be treated as a cost center. You need to demonstrate not only each component, but also the line-item expenses of planning and implementing each component. This applies to every component with the exception of the environmental scan and the lead and sales objectives.

Take your manpower requirements, for example. You'll need to identify base salaries, commissions and benefits, and any educational and training costs (from conference fees to consulting support). When it comes to special events, how many are planned for the year, and what are the costs to host and promote the programs, from refreshments and equipment to direct mail and print promotions? Your collateral materials account needs to detail each item and planned quantities, and distinguish the cost of design and production from that of printing. Direct mail, print media, and electronic media (if used) require extensive cost detail. For instance, what are the line-item costs for design, production, printing, list, label, and postage for each direct mail campaign? What is the cost of your print media plan, from the expense of designing and producing each ad to media buys?

The *Marketing Plan Template* contains a Prototype Marketing Budget you can follow to compile your program expenses. You'll then need to work with finance and accounting to determine how your marketing budget will interface with the organization's budget (in format, automation, and expense reporting).

You also want to make sure you're in on the budget reporting loop so that you can simultaneously monitor two performance standards: 1) projected-to-actual expenses, and 2) actual expenses in relation to the achievement of your lead and sales objectives. This must happen every month, so that you can correct any planned to actual program deviations.

Conclusion

That's it. That's how marketing works.

At this point, I'm supposed to provide a provocative summary of the book's content, and direct you to the *Marketing Plan Template* on CD that will take you through the next steps. Instead, I want to share a final piece of advice.

While writing this book, I reflected on all the communities I worked with and all the lessons I learned. Over the years, I came to realize that the formula for marketing isn't complicated. It only gets complicated when folks don't follow the formula. Marketing success has less to do with the arrangement of external parts, and more to do with you, the practitioner.

Ours is a special profession, a vocation really, where skill merges with a mission of service. With a vocation, there is no division between who you are and what you do for a living. *Inside Advice on Marketing Senior Housing* provides you with the tools of the trade; it's up to you to perfect your work principles. Set and strive for high standards. Pursue a purposeful path and approach it with a passion. Be determined to make a difference. Grow your skills so you can plan with confidence and implement with ease. Grow yourself so that you positively influence the lives of those you serve. Do your work with all your heart, and you will succeed. There is so little competition.

Phyllis M. Thornton

INDEX

A
Active lead, 61
Active lead base, 24
Advertising
    brand advertising, 111–112
    call to action in, 101
    function of, 129
    integration of components, 100–102
    prerequisites, 130–131
    print materials. *See* Collateral materials
    of special events, 97–98, 100
    to market service area, 5
Advertising flights, 138, 147
Affinity groups, assessing, 9
Age demographic, 7
    younger, attracting, 7
Age-bias
    copywriting, 106-107
    event themes, 96–97
    "old folks' home," 104, 108
    phrases, 105
    positioning, 98
    products, 108
Aged population. *See also* Senior consumers
    effect on younger crowd, 7
Amenities, presentation in printed materials, 121
Analysis
    attrition, 21
    geographic origin, 5
    lead-to-sale close rate, 26–27
    competitive, 10
    consumer analysis tools, 8–9
    cost-per-lead rate, 29–30
    cost-per-sale rate, 29–30
    industry-average costing ratios, 30
    lead count, 23
    lead and sales source, 24–25
    lead source forecasts, 29
    lead-to-tour rate, 29
    optional steps, 29
    organizational strengths, 12
    organizational weaknesses, 12–13
    product, service, price, 13
    tour-to-sale rate, 29

Apartments
    market-ready, 19–20, 77
    model, ideal, 74
    resident vs model, the use of, 74–75
    selling techniques, 77–78
    showing to prospects, 76–78
Application, presentation in printed materials, 121
Attrition
    actionable information, translating data into, 18
    fluctuations of, 20–21
    projecting, 20–22

B

Base salary, 52
Billboard advertising, 146
Board members, referral generation from, 86–87
Brand advertising, 111–112
Broadcast advertising. *See* Electronic media
Budget, marketing, 167-168
Budgetary assumptions, 167
Budgetary planning process, 167–168
Business etiquette, staff training in, 40

C

Calibrated marketing for events, 99–100
Caregiver, marketing to
    educational programs, 95
    e-mail, 142
    information resource, 158
    radio, 156
CDs or DVDs
    collateral, 125–126
    sales tool, 74
Celebrity appearances at special events, 96
Chronic vacancies, 6
Close rate
    analyzing, 26–27
    lead objective and, 27–28
    low or declining, 26–27
    projected, 26
Collateral materials, 115–127
    application and contract documents, 121
    CD or DVD, 125–126
    consistency among, 118
    cost control, 126–127
    effectiveness of, 115
    electronic, 74
    floor plans, 120
    graphic portfolio, signature of, 118
    inserts, 119–122
    introductory brochures, 122–123

Index 173

    marketing newsletter, 123–125
    price sheets, 121
    primary information brochure, 116–119
    quality of, 117
    services and amenities listing, 121
    stationery package, 123
    time spent creating versus generating leads, 115–116
Commissions, 52–53
    salary versus commission philosophies, 52
    average ranges, 53
    scale, 53
    override, 53
Commission Scale, 53
Commission Scale table, 53
Communication integration, 100–102
    advertising/event frequency, 147
    advertising strategy, 154
    CD and DVD, 125
    direct mail, 134
    e-mail, 142
    graphic portfolio, 118
    marketing components, 131
    marketing programs, 46
    newsletter, 125
    print communications, 116
    strategic networking, 81, 90, 101
    sustained interest, 69
    themes, 147
    time lines, 165
Communities
    market demand for, 67–68
    naming issues, 108
    physical appearance of, 13, 36–37
    Web sites for, 157–158
Community Affairs, 81
Community Affairs Representative role, 44
Compensation of staff, 52–53
Competition
    collateral materials and documents of, studying, 11
    market-share competition, 10
    mind-share competition, 10
    occupancy at expense of, 11
    occupancy rates, comparing, 11
    researching, 10–12
    weaknesses of, capitalizing on, 11–12
Competitive audit, 10
Competitor Provider Profile, 10
Congregate housing, 6
Consumer-analysis tools, 8–9
Contact methods, identifying in prospect record, 59

Contracts, presentation in printed materials, 121
Copywriting
　crafting right message, 106–108
　industry jargon, institutional phrases to avoid, 107–108
Costing ratios, industry-average, 30
Cost-per-lead, 29–30
Cost-per-sale, 29–30
Cost-per-unit, 29–30
Creative design and copywriting, 105–112
　branding, 111–122
　images and icons, 110–111
　defined, 105
　graphic elements, 109–111
Creative themes
　for direct mail, 138
　for print media, 147–148, 150
　for special events, 96–97
Cross-marketing, 97
Customer point of view, assessing community from, 13
Customer service, 33–41
　concepts of, 34–40
　marketing contribution to, 40–41
　physical plant, 36–37
　protocols in, defining, 40–41
　staff appearance, 38–39
　staff attitudes and actions, 39–40
　telephone reception, 35–36
　training programs in, 40–41

D

Decision influencers, seminar marketing to, 94–95
Demographic profile
　age upon entering community, 7
　determining, 6–7
　income target, 7
Demographics
　defined, 6
　MKIS data category, 57–58
Direct mail, 24, 135–142
　benefits of, 135–136
　delivery logistics, 140–141
　design of, 140
　effectiveness of, 132–133
　electronic mail, 142
　flights, 138
　mailings, maximizing, 140–142
　mail list, 137
　marketing matrix for, 138–139
　materials, theme-based, 138
　planning campaign, 136–138
　rate of return, 139–140
　reach, 137

seasonal influences, 141–142
   timing of, 138
   tips on, 141–142
Direct Mail Marketing Matrix, 139
Direct Mail Planner, 136, 138
Directories, 146
Disposition of leads, 60–61
Dress code, staff, 38–39

E
Educational events, 94–95
Education of staff, 49–51
Electronic collateral materials, 74, 125–126
Electronic mail, 142
Electronic media, 24, 153–158
   frequency and duration of, 155
   for public relations, 154–155
   plan for, 155–156
   suitability of, 154–155
   tips on, 155–156
   Web advertising, 156–158
Environment
   imperfections in, identifying and fixing, 36–37
   understanding, 3
Environmental scan, 3–4
   internal assessment, 12–15
   internal strengths and weaknesses, assessing, 12–15
   market area, defining, 4–5
   of competition, assessing, 10–12
   target market, defining, 6–9
Event marketing, 93
   calibrated marketing for, 99–100
Event promotions, 97–98
Event themes, 96

F
Financial accountability, 168
Financial program
   assessing, 13–14
   real versus perceived problems with, 14
First impressions, managing, 35–36
Floor plans, presentation in printed materials, 120–121
Focus group surveys, 9
Follow-up
   lead management protocols, 65
   Lead-Management Protocols, sample of, 65
   staff resistance to, 66
   timing of, 61
Frontline staff. *See also* Staff
   customer service, understanding of and expertise in, 33–34
Futures list, 67–69

G

Gantt, 164-166
Gantt Chart, Marketing Manpower, 165
Geographic Origin Analysis table, 5
Geography of market service area, 4
Graphic design
    casting the community, 110–111
    of marketing communications, 109–111
    use of models, 110
Graphic portfolio for marketing materials, 118–119
Grass roots networking, 81–91
Growth marketing strategy
    defined, 30, 99
    direct mail marketing for, 137–138
    event marketing strategies for, 99–100
    print media advertising, 146–147
    staffing for, 44

H

Housekeeping, quality of, 13, 37

I

Inactive lead, 61
Inactive leads, 63
Incentive programs
    for move-ins, 84–85
    for referrals, 84
    for staff, 53
Income target demographic, 7
Information architecture, 57–62
    demographics data, 57–58
    marketing data, 59–62
    psychographic data, 58–59
    sales data, 62
Information-based decision making, 55
Information center and resources, 71–78
    apartment showings, 76–78
    accessories and appointments of, 73
    centralized, 74
    converting vacant units to, 74
    equipment, 74
    furnishings, 72–73
    model apartment, 74–76
    multi-suite sales environment, 73–74
    single suite sales environment, 72–73
Inquiry-to-close rate, 26–27
Inserts, 119–122
Internal assessment, 12–15
    strengths, identifying, 12
Internet advertising, 156–158
Introductory brochures, 122–123

L

Lead and Sales Objectives Summary table, 29
Lead and sales source
    identifying in the MKIS, 59
    paid, 24
    referral-based, 24
Lead and Sales Source Analysis table, 23–25
Lead Count Analysis table, 23
Lead count, qualified, defined, 24
Lead count total, defined, 23
Lead-management procedures, 62–67
    prospect procedures, 64–67
    sample procedures, 65
    software protocols, 63
Lead-Management Protocols, sample of, 65
Lead-management software, 56
Lead objective, 19, 22–29
    calculating, 27
    close rate and, 27–28
    defined, 26
    lead and sales source, 24–25
    lead count, 23–24
    lead-to-sale close rate, 26–27
    net lead objective, 28
    projected close rate and, 26
Lead Objective table, 28
Lead source
    analysis of, 24–25
    forecasting, 29
    paid, 24
    referral-based, 24
    segmenting leads by, 24
    versus sales source, 25
Lead status, identifying in the MKIS, 59–62
Lead-to-Sale Close Rate table, 26
Lead-to-tour rate, analyzing, 29
Leads
    active versus inactive, 60–61
    disposition of, 60–61
    qualified, 60
    from referral-based marketing versus paid media, 82
    sales generation from, 18–19

M

Mail list, direct mail, 137
Mail list, generating from lead-management software, 62–63
Mail surveys, 8–9
Maintenance, quality of, 13, 37
Maintenance marketing strategy
    defined, 30, 99

    direct mail marketing for, 137–138
    event-marketing strategies for, 99–100
    print media advertising, 145, 147
    staffing for, 45
Major dailies, 146
Manners, staff training in, 40
Manpower Gantt Chart, 166
Marketing
    MKIS data category, 59
    smart marketing, 17–18
    strategic mind-set in, 4
    superior communities versus superior sales staff, 12
    team approach, 45
Marketing and sales manpower, 43–53
    compensation of, 52–53
    functions of, 44–45
    performance, optimizing, 46–47
    productivity and performance goals, 47–48
    staffing configurations and capacity, 48–49
    training and education, 49–51
Marketing Assistant role, 44
Marketing audit
    benefits of, 18
    defined, 18
Marketing barriers
    causes of, 13
    effect on sales, quantifying, 14
    identifying, 12–13
    real versus perceived, 14
Marketing budget, 167–168
Marketing communications. *See also* Direct mail; Electronic media; Print media
    age bias in, 105
    graphic design of, 109–111
Marketing components
    administrative aspect, 161
    budgeting by, 167–168
    customer service line up, 33
    defined, 31
    lower-cost versus paid, 31, 131
    marketing tactics, 31
    networking component, 81. *See also* Strategic networking
    public relations, 89
    quality customer service, 41
Marketing data in the MKIS, 59–62
Marketing department
    customer service protocols, defining, 40–41
    role of, 163
    workplace, descriptive term for, 71
    workplace, physical setting of, 72
Marketing director, 44
    commission of, 53

growth marketing strategy, 44
  improving sales practices, 63
  marketing program, 22
  networking responsibilities, 45, 83, 90
  paid media, using, 132
  performance goals, 48
  time management, 46
Marketing implementation, time spent on, 46–47
Marketing information, pacing with inserts, 119–122
Marketing information system (MKIS), 9, 55–69
  accessing response rates, 59, 149
  as a consumer-analysis tool, 9
  assimilating data, 55
  information architecture, 57–62
  lead-management procedures, 62–67
  lead-management software, 56
  marketing data, 59
  outside expert installation of, 67
  psychographics, 58
  resident contributions to, 85
  sales data, 62
  wait-list, 67–69
Marketing logistics, 130–131
Marketing newsletter, 123–125. *See also* Newsletters
  content of, 124
  functions of, 123
  publication frequency, 125
  resident profiles in, 124
Marketing objectives and strategy
  lead objective, 22–29
  occupancy principle, 18–19
  quantifying, 30–31
  sales objective, 19–22
  setting, 18–31
  summary of, 29–30
Marketing plan, 161–166
  budget, 167–168
  goals, objectives, strategy, and tactics elements, 164
  lead objective, 22–29
  politics of, 162–163
  proactive, 162
  sales objective, 19–22, 29
  shape and intensity of, 18
  template for, 163–166
  time line, 164–166
  time spent on, 46–47
Marketing Plan Template, 5, 163–168
  Competitor Provider Profile, 10
  customer service action steps, 41
  Direct Mail Planner, 136, 138

Geographic Origin Analysis table, 5
Gantt Chart, 166
Lead and Sales Objectives Summary table, 29
Lead and Sales Source Analysis table, 23–25
Lead Count Analysis table, 23
lead-management software, using with, 56
Lead-to-Sale Close Rate table, 26
Move-In and Attrition Analysis table, 20
Net Lead Objective table, 29
Print Media Plan, 150
Prototype Marketing Budget, 168
Sales Performance Goals table, 47–48
Special Events Planner, 99
Strategic Networking Planner, 83
Marketing program
  components of, 31, 131, 167–168
  marketing and sales functions, 44–45
  public relations and, 89
  shape and intensity of, 18
  situation-driven versus market-driven, 162
  time frame for, 164–166
  track of, assessing, 18
Marketing strategy, defined, 30
Marketing tactics, defined, 31
Marketing videos or DVDs, 74, 125–126
Market-ready apartments, 19–20, 77
Market service area
  defining, 4–5
  direct mail, use in, 137
  inclusion, key for, 5
  neighborhood affiliation and, 4
  predatory competition and, 4
  reach and penetration in, 5
  targeting, 5
  topographical boundaries of, 4
  updating data on, 5
Market-share, fighting for, 11
Market-share competition, 10
  defined, 10
Mass-market advertising. *See* Electronic media
Master planning process, marketing and sales team input in, 15
Media, networking with, 89–90
Media outlets, researching, 150
Media performance, tracking and analyzing, 151
Mind-share competition, 10
Model apartment
  resident's apartment versus model, 74–75
  standards for, 75–76
Move-In and Attrition Analysis table, 20
Move-in coordinator role, 44

Move-in data, translating into actionable information, 18
Move-in incentives, 84–85
Move-ins
    attrition analysis, and, 21
    fluctuations of, 20–21
    occupancy determination from, 18–19
    from sales, 18–19

N
Neighborhood affiliation, 4
Neighborhood publications, 146
Net lead objective, 28–29
Net Lead Objective table, 29
Networking. *See also* Strategic networking
    defined, 81
Newsletters. *See also* Marketing newsletter
    appeal and quality of, 101
    reply coupon in, 101
Newspaper advertising. *See also* Print Media
    design of and copy in, 101
    effectiveness of, 132–133
    frequency of, 101

O
Objectives
    defined, 18
    quantifiable, 18
Occupancy
    commissions and compensation tied to, 53
    goals, determining, 18–19
    goals, obtaining, 17
    marketing plan, 164
    vacancies, chronic, 11
Occupancy principle, 18–19
Outreach efforts. *See also* Strategic networking
    to market service area, 5
    phone calls, 88
    to primary focus markets, 84–87
    to secondary focus markets, 87–88
    speaker's bureau for, 89
    steps to, 88

P
Paid media, 129–133
    case against, 131–132
    price-to-value relationship, 132–133
    readiness for, 130–131
    versus referral-based marketing, 82
Partnering with businesses, 97
Performance goals for marketing and sales team, 47–48
Performance targets, close rate, 26
Personal service
    for telephone reception, 35–36
    staff training for, 39–40

Phone books, advertising in, 148
Phone surveys, 8–9
Physical plant, 36–37
    product assessment, 13
    standards of excellence for, defining, 37
Point of contact service quality of competition, 11
Prerequisites-to-Advertising-Success Quiz, 130–131
Prescreening process, 7
Price assessment, 13
Price marketing barriers, 13
Price points, assessing, 13
Pricing information
    conveying, 121–122
    presentation in printed materials, 121–122
Primary focus markets
    board members, 86–87
    networking with, 84–87
    prospects, 85–86
    residents, 84–85
    residents' family and friends, 86
    staff members, 86–87
    volunteers, 86–87
    wait-list, 85–86
Primary information brochure, 116–119
    design specifications for, 117–118
    graphic portfolio in, 118–119
    quality of, 117
Print materials. *See* Collateral materials
Print media, 24, 145–151
    action steps for, 150–151
    ad design, 147
    elements of, 146–148
    in media-intense environments, 148–149
    intensity and frequency of, 148–149
    placement and frequency, 145
    plan for, 150–151
    response rate, 149
    strategy for, defining, 150
    themes of, 147–148
Product assessment, 13
Productivity goals for marketing and sales team, 47–48
    monthly phone calls, 48
    monthly sales, 48
Product marketing barriers, 13
Product repositioning, considering, 11, 14–15
Programs, naming versus labeling, 108
Projected close rate, 26
Promotional materials. *See also* Advertising; Collateral materials
    integration of, 100–102
Promotional plan

networking, 81–91
special events, 93–102
Promotion of special events, 93–102
Prospect base, 24
Prospect objections, 13, 14, 49, 51, 61, 62, 78, 103, 122
Prospect record
demographics data, 57–58
information in, 57
marketing data, 59–62
psychographics data, 58–59
sales data, 62
Prospects. *See also* Senior consumers
decision-making support for, 85
direct mail marketing to, 140
information about, 57–62
interactions with, 48
networking with, 85–86
objections versus occupancy impediments, 13
perception of communities, 105
transactions with, recording, 62
Prototype Marketing Budget, 168
Psychographics
analysis of, 8–9
MKIS data category 58–59
profile of target market, 8–9
Public relations
defined, 89
networking and, 89–90
Public service announcements, electronic media for, 154–155

Q

Qualified lead count, defined, 24
Qualified leads, defined, 60
Quality of service, customer judgment of, 34
Quantifiable objectives, formulating, 18

R

Radio advertising. *See also* Electronic media
effectiveness of, 132–133
Referral-based marketing versus paid media, 82
Referral programs
incentives for, 84
resident involvement in, 84–85
Referral sources
analysis of, 24
list management, 88
MKIS coding, 59
sample list of, 87
Repositioning, 11
prerequisites for, 15
unsuccessful strategies, 14

Reservation list, 67–69
Resident profiles, demographic information in, 6–7
Residents
    geographic origin of, 4
    referral programs, participation in, 84–85,
Residents' families and friends, networking with, 86
Resident surveys, 9
Resident testimonials, 84
Resources
    budgeting for, 167
    information center, 74
    securing, 163
Response rate
    of direct mail campaigns, 139–140
    of print media, 149
    MKIS, program assessment, 59, 149

S

Sales
    generating from leads, 18–19
    generating move-ins from, 18–19
    incompetent practices, 26–27
Sales data
    actionable information, translating into, 18
    in prospect record, 62
Sales environment
    apartment showings, 76–78
    model apartment, 74–76
    multi-suite, 73–74
    privacy of, 72
    single suite, 72–73
Sales managers, commissions of, 53
Sales objective, 19–22
    attrition and, 20–21
    information trending, 21–22
    sales formula for, 22
    vacant units and, 19–20
Sales Objective table, 22
Sales performance goals, 48
Sales representatives
    commissions, 52
    goals of, 47
    information center, setting up, 72–74
    lead-management protocols and, 66
    lead-to-sale close rate, 27
    marketing assistant support, 45
    monthly phone calls, 48
    monthly sales, 48
    presenting their communities, 36
    prospect procedures for, 65–66
    relationship building and discovery, 119

role of, 44
staffing your program with, 167
time allocation, 46–47
Sales source
analysis of, 24–25
perpetuating, 25
versus lead source, 25
Sales tasks, time spent on, 47
Sales team production, gauging, 26
Sample Commission Scale, 53
Sample Lead-Management Protocols, 65
Sample Training Session Outline, 65
Saturated markets, occupancy at competition's expense, 11
Secondary focus markets, networking with, 87–88
Seminars, 94
Senior consumers
age-biased products, dislike of, 108
direct mail, preference for, 136
electronic media and, 155
marketing messages that appeal to, 107
Senior market
staff readiness to work with, 49
targeting, 6–8
Service assessment, 13
Service excellence
pursuit of, 34
staff training for, 35
Service marketing barriers, 13
Services
assessing, 13–14
emphasis in marketing communications, 106
fixing, 15
move-in services, 85
presentation in printed materials, 121
Social programs, 95
Speaker's bureau, 89
Special events marketing, 24, 93–102
communication integration, 100–102
defined, 97
educational events, 94–95
execution of, 102
goal of, 93
marketing matrix for, 99–100
media promotion of, 97–98
social programs, 95
themes, imaginative, 96–97
Special Events Marketing Matrix, 98–99
Special Events Planner, 99
Special-interest sectors, psychographics data on, 58
Specialty publications, 146

Specific, Measurable, Achievable, Realistic, and Timely (SMART) path, 30
Staff. *See also* Marketing and sales manpower
    actions and attitudes of, 34, 39–40
    appearance of, 38–39
    base salary for, 52
    commissions for, 52–53
    configuration and capacity, 48–49
    housekeeping and maintenance responsibilities of, 37
    referral generation from, 86–87
    training and education of, 49–51
Staff Peformance Goals and Capacity table, 48
Stationery package, 123
Strategic mind-set, 4
Strategic networking, 81–91
    board members, 86–87
    deferral of, 83
    networking with, 84–87
    plan for, 83–84
    primary focus markets, 84–87
    prospects, 85–86
    public relations, 89–90
    residents, 84–85
    residents' family and friends, 86
    roles, goals, and performance standards, 90–91
    secondary focus markets, 87–88
    speaker's bureau, 89
    staff members, 86–87
    value of, 82–83
    vigorousness of, 82
    volunteers, 86–87
    wait-list, 85–86
Strategic Networking Planner, 83
Strengths, identifying, 12
Strengths, weaknesses, opportunities, and threats (SWOT) analysis, 3
Survey research
    focus group surveys, 9
    mail and phone surveys, 8–9
    Marketing Information System (MKIS), 9
    resident surveys, 9
SWOT analysis, 3

T
Tangible benefits, assessing, 13
Target market
    defining, 6–8
    demographic profile of, 6–7
    needs and desires, knowing, 6
    psychographic profile of, 8–9
Team approach to marketing, 45
Telemarketing performance goals, 48

Telephone directories, advertising in, 148
Telephone reception, 35–36
   hours of, 36
   staffing of, 36
   staff training in, 36
   voice mail and, 35–36
Television advertising. *See also* Electronic media
   effectiveness of, 132–133
Testimonials, 84
Time line of marketing program, 164–166
Topics of special events, 96–97
Total lead count, defined, 23
Touring performance goals, assigning, 48
Tour-to-close rate, analyzing, 29
Training of staff, 49–51
   industry marketing consultant firm for, 50–51
   resources for, 50
   Sample Session Outline for,
      Trend analysis, 21–22

U
Unique Selling Proposition (USP), identifying, 12
Unit count, market-ready versus community units, 19–20
Unit Count Recap table, 19–20
Unit mix, assessing, 13–14
Units
   market-ready, 19–20, 77
   size, assessing, 13–14

V
Vacancies, chronic, 11
Visuals, unification of, 100–101
Voice mail, senior consumers and, 35–36
Volunteers, referral generation from, 86–87

W
Wait-list
   advantage of, 67
   culling, 68–69
   direct mail marketing to, 140
   disadvantages of, 67–68
   integrity of, 68
   managing and marketing, 67–69
   networking with, 85–86
Web-based advertising, 24. *See also* Electronic media
Web page design, 157–158
Word of mouth, 24
Working lead base, 24
Workshops, 94

Inside Advice On
MARKETING SENIOR HOUSING

MARKETING PLAN TEMPLATE

This book is furnished with a CD that contains the following information:

Marketing Plan Template: for creating your own marketing plan, or to strengthen a program that you already have in place. The Template follows the 15 critical components of marketing and allows you to customize information to your community, as well as produce a working plan prototype that you can use time and again.

Template Instructions and Action Steps: for detailed guidance, tables, worksheets, and planners to complete the Marketing Plan Template and draft your plan.

Additional Information Resources: for training and certification programs, recommended firms that offer marketing services and products, and information on purchasing additional copies of the book and CD.